# LANDSCAPES

# OF CHANGE

ROXI THOREN

# LANDSCAPES

# OF CHANGE

## INNOVATIVE DESIGNS
## AND REINVENTED SITES

**TIMBER PRESS**
PORTLAND — LONDON

To Jamie, Ellie, and Jeb

Frontispiece: A viewing platform at Jaffa Landfill Park connects city, sea, and history.

Copyright © 2014 by Roxi Thoren. All rights reserved.
Published in 2014 by Timber Press, Inc.

The Haseltine Building
133 S.W. Second Avenue, Suite 450
Portland, Oregon 97204-3527
timberpress.com

6a Lonsdale Road
London NW6 6RD
timberpress.co.uk

Image credits appear on page 257.
Printed in China
Text design by Stacy Wakefield
Cover design by Patrick Barber and Stacy Wakefield

Library of Congress Cataloging-in-Publication Data

Thoren, Roxi.
Landscapes of change: innovative designs and reinvented sites/Roxi Thoren.—First edition.
       pages cm
   Includes bibliographical references and index.
   ISBN 978-1-60469-386-7
   1. Landscape architecture—Case studies. 2. Reclamation of land—Case studies. I. Title.
   SB472.T485 2014
   712—dc23                                          2014014442

A catalog record for this book is also available from the British Library.

Like books, landscapes can be read, but unlike
books, they were not meant to be read.

—Peirce Lewis

# CONTENTS

## ECOLOGICAL URBANISM
**156** Design Informed by Natural Systems

## EDIBLE LANDSCAPES
**204** Agriculture in the City

Introduction

# INDELIBLE SOCIAL MARKS

Recent decades have seen a burgeoning of innovation in landscape architecture. Designers have explored material possibilities, from reused site materials at the low end to technologically sophisticated components at the high end. Hybrid projects have synthesized multiple disciplines, including architecture and art, engineering and ecology. Designers have expanded their vocabulary of forms, translating practices from different fields into landscape process and pattern. And there have been new design processes, including new modes of community-based design, self-funding projects, and projects that generate their own materials over time. In no small part, these innovations arise from

Public Farm 1 in Queens, New York: Urban agriculture is among several physical and conceptual sites inspiring landscape architects in recent decades.

—

**9**

opportunities inherent in the kinds of sites landscape architects are being asked to design on and for. This book provides a framework for understanding and critiquing contemporary landscape practice, a framework based in the material, ecological, and social sites of projects, and in the tactics designers use when defining and expressing those sites.

Some of the changing context of landscape architectural design is internal to the profession, as designers increasingly explore material processes, seek a theoretical basis internal to the discipline, embrace a landscape praxis of (in the words of Paulo Freire) "reflection and action upon the world in order to transform it," and engage the challenges and opportunities of complex, multidisciplinary projects. But much of the changed context is external to the profession, as social, economic, and climatic conditions, values, and perceptions shift. Many factors are currently influencing design: urban growth in some regions (more than half the world's population lived in an urban center in 2008, for the first time in human history) and urban decay in others (Detroit being a notable example), population growth that is stressing natural resources, and the global reorganization of industry. These forces have left urban sites open for redevelopment at a time when cities are demanding parks, streets, and plazas that perform environmental and ecological as well as social functions. At the same time, undeniable changes in global weather patterns have led to an increased demand for landscapes that are resilient in the face of storms, flooding, or drought.

Urban populations have demanded new forms of open space and new connections to natural amenities. At the same time, changes in infrastructure and industry have opened new types of sites for parks and other open space. Industry has largely left our downtowns; residents have demanded that roads and rail lines connect instead of divide cities, or even serve as amenities; environmental function has become a priority; and city residents are calling for local food options. These factors have led to the rediscovery and reinvention of urban sites as complex hybrids that perform multiple functions.

Scholars and practitioners of landscape architecture have grappled with explaining and responding to this shifting context and its resultant designs. In recent decades, we have articulated a slew of urbanisms—new, landscape, infrastructural, ecological, combinatory, weak, opportunistic, deep, tactical. We have also seen more broadly defined design theories—post-Fordist, postindustrial, postmodern. This semantic difficulty highlights how significantly the context of design has shifted in recent years, and how landscape theory has struggled to catch up to the dynamic and thrilling innovations in practice.

Yet many of the innovative tactics that landscape architects are employing

hearken back to the roots of the profession and to deeply placeful design. The anonymous development of cities such as Venice and New Orleans took advantage of the ecological and systemic site. Venice sits at the confluence of riparian and marine systems; historically, the interwoven stream channels were used as transportation and sewage infrastructure, and sites for collecting potable rainwater were an urban design tactic, generating neighborhood piazzas where residents met daily. Similarly, New Orleans sits at the meeting point of two key transportation infrastructures: the Mississippi River and the Gulf of Mexico. The historic long lots of the city provided each landowner with transportation connections and an ecological transect of the region, from raised river to sunken bayou. This mode of design continued through the nineteenth century, with the technological and infrastructural designs of Alphand and Olmsted. Our contemporary infrastructure projects show similar creativity with different technology.

Every work of landscape architecture simultaneously is somewhere and is about something. Landscape architects define these two sites—the physical and the discursive—in their design process. After a century of increased specialization, landscape architects are returning to the site itself as a source of material, technological, and infrastructural innovation. Elizabeth Meyer has said, "Defining the site is a creative act, undertaken by an architect or landscape architect during the early process of design." This book limns the categories of sites that landscape architects are defining for themselves in contemporary practice. It examines the role that new sites—both physical and conceptual—have in design innovation. Infrastructure, postindustrial sites, vegetated architecture, urban ecology, and urban

Buffalo Bayou Promenade in Houston, Texas: The park hybridizes stormwater infrastructure, recreation, and ecological restoration.

**11**

Northala Fields Park
in London, England:
The designers used the
processes of construction
and demolition as
the foundation for
self-funding land art.

12

agriculture have each been discussed individually and extensively as movements in the profession or society, but not as expressions of a common situation. This book provides a critical and theoretical framework for understanding these recent trends in landscape architecture as branch expressions from a common root.

The book is structured by sites and tactics. The five categories of sites explored here are renewed areas of exploration for landscape architects and divide into physical and conceptual sites. Infrastructure, postindustrial sites, and vegetated buildings are all actual places—physical forms or histories of sites. Agriculture is a conceptual site: while agricultural practices certainly have physical forms, patterns, and alignments, agriculture isn't a physical aspect or pre-occupation of a site per se but instead a way of conceiving a site, of integrating food, soil, and habitat production into design thinking. Ecology is a hybrid—part physical site, part conceptual. The composition, structure, and function of environmental and ecological systems pre-occupy sites, through geomorphology, surficial and subsurficial water movement, and habitat structure, among other systems. But while one cannot ignore the physical nature of designing on infrastructure, on a factory site, or on a building, ecological structure can be, and often is, ignored. There is, therefore, a conceptual aspect to the ecological site, a need for the designer to *want* to engage with ecosystem function.

With the exception of postindustrial sites, all of these kinds of sites are more a recovery of the synthetic nature of landscape architecture than an *ex novo* innovation in the field. Ecology pertains to first nature—wild nature, untouched by human activity; agriculture and infrastructure are forms of second nature—human-cultivated land made culturally productive. And vegetated architecture has roots in the third nature of the hanging gardens of Babylon and the turf houses of medieval Scandinavia. In many ways, the innovation we see is a return to sources, a recovery of the processes of landscapes themselves, and a reinvestigation of the depth of sites—both physically and culturally. By peeling up and digging down, designers are recovering the thick agency of landscapes.

The projects in this book—twenty-five designs in twelve countries—were selected to represent the breadth of tactics used in perceiving, critiquing, and designing with the opportunities and constraints that the five categories of site provide. Many of the projects exploit more than one kind of site in their designs. Queens Plaza, for instance, engages both infrastructure and ecology; Péage Sauvage explores both ecology and postindustrial conditions. And a sixth, invisible kind of site flows through the book: the material site. Nearly all of the projects explore the production, disposal, and reuse of materials as an aspect of their design. Materials are reused on-site, as in the concrete at Queens Plaza and the asphalt at the Kroc Center. They are used site-to-site, with demolition and reclamation materials both imported, at Northala Fields, or exported, at Jaffa Landfill Park. At the Marco Polo Airport car park, trees are moved and removed in a movable nursery, with time—that primary material of landscape architecture—conceived as a resource. The projects within each chapter were selected to provide an overlapping view of the kind of site being analyzed. Some of the projects are very well known, others are less so; together they provide a robust range of design responses to and interventions into that kind of site.

Because this book explores the precondition of the site as a design generator, each project is described through its site history. The narratives describe the projects as interventions into already existing sets of physical, material, ecological, and cultural processes. While many of the innovations are in the designs, for several projects the innovations are in the process of design (Beacon Food Forest, Prinzessinnengarten) or construction (Northala Fields), or in the growth and mutability of the project after construction (Marco Polo Airport car park).

Art critic Miwon Kwon has argued that digging into sites, metaphorically, conceptually, allows us to connect to places with "relational specificity." She says, "Only those cultural practices that have this relational sensibility can turn local encounters into long-term commitments and transform passing intimacies into indelible, unretractable social marks." The projects presented here are indicative of that trend in landscape architecture, a movement away from passing intimacies, quick engagements with distant sites, and toward local, specific, contingent, and enduring designs—indelible social marks.

# INFRASTRUCTURE
## Rethinking Public Works

Solar Strand in
Amherst, New York.

**LANDSCAPE ARCHITECTURE** was conceived as a synthetic discipline. In the early years of the profession, farming, timber production, hydrologic engineering, bridges, and roads were all within the purview of the landscape architect. Projects by Frederick Law Olmsted, such as the Back Bay Fens in Boston, used the exigencies of urban life as a catalyst for innovative design. Writing about the project in 1886, Olmsted listed, in order of significance, four reasons for the construction of the Fens: sanitation, transportation, bank stabilization, and finally, "a general scheme of sylvan improvement for the city," but only inasmuch as it was required by the first three goals and could be accomplished "thriftily." What is now seen as a natural area and public park was designed as sanitation and transportation infrastructure.

Olmsted went on to write:

> The professional fields respectively of the Architect, the Engineer, the Sanitary Engineer and the Landscape Gardener or Landscape Architect are in the main well-defined. Yet, at certain points, one merges into the other in such a manner that they may be regarded as so many convenient subdivisions of one field and each profession as a branch of one trunk profession. You see engineering journals giving plans of buildings, and architectural journals discussing plans of drainage of bridges and of parks. But as yet there is much (less) disposition to ready and cordial cooperation between these branch professions than is desirable for the public interests.

Nearly 130 years later, we face the same challenge and the same opportunity. Cities arose as sites of exchange: exchange of knowledge, materials, power, people. For the city to survive, life-supporting systems are needed: water, food, and waste. Production, exchange, consumption, and waste have a structure, in the pipes and wires over our heads and beneath our feet; in tunnels, roads, bridges, canals; in factories, server farms, and landfills. As Gary Strang noted, "The machine is not so much in the garden as it is indistinguishable from the garden; they are inexorably intertwined." The infrastructures of the city are ubiquitous, and during the twentieth century, they were largely designed by engineers for the most efficient function of a single purpose, whether conveying vehicles from place to place or producing electricity. Now infrastructure is experiencing a design renaissance: symposia, books, and themed journals have all been dedicated to the topic in recent years.

These life-supporting systems provide both new sites of design and new ways of designing. We are seeing creative new treatments of the sites of transportation, communication, energy and food production, and water and waste storage and handling. The sites themselves often provide new areas for habitat and open space within the city. Layered sites are somewhat common; Lawrence Halprin's Freeway Park in Seattle, completed in 1976, is an early example of constructing landscape over infrastructure. More nuanced and rewarding are hybrid sites, which accommodate both technical and social programs in the same territory. They challenge the designer and reward the citizen with opportunities to see and interact with the systems that make urban life possible. So many of the systems we rely on are invisible: water flows when we turn the tap and lights glow when we flip a switch. This disconnect between system design and resource use generates indifference and ignorance; we cannot care about that which we do not see.

A new parking lot at the Venice Marco Polo Airport considers that most ubiquitous and banal of urban spaces as a site with material, environmental, and social potential, a place of possible beauty that could counter the disorientation visitors often experience as they attempt to relocate their cars. The project hybridizes the abstract metrics of car size and turning radii with an existing woodland. The interaction of the two systems creates the structure for a brightly colored, meandering path through the vast parking lot that provides shade and orientation. The project also anticipates the growth of the airport with a moving nursery strategy. Removed trees are replanted in open meadows to continue growing and contributing to the ecosystem. When new construction requires trees, they can be taken from the nursery, and when the field is needed for expansion, the nursery can move again.

In Moses Bridge, infrastructure considers its own history and questions normative solutions to infrastructural problems. The bridge, carved through the waters of a moat, provides access to a fort that was once part of Holland's water defense system. Under attack, a 20,000-acre area could be flooded via water gates and locks to stop the advance of enemy troops. The water that perennially threatens Holland was turned into a defensive infrastructure. The bridge effects a similar inversion: rather than bridging over the moat, it slices through it, and in cutting the water, it protects the historic appearance of the fort. The project questions the fundamental definition of an infrastructure element: Must a bridge always go over? Or must it simply connect across a barrier?

Queens Plaza in New York takes a traffic engineering problem and turns it into a social and ecological site, showing that urban transportation infrastructures can be productive. The new plaza and streetscape is one of New York City's High Performance Infrastructure projects and aims to be a model for transportation infrastructure that also provides social areas and enhances the environment. The project captures and filters all storm water, both improving water quality before it enters the East River and providing rainwater storage capacity that can alleviate flooding in future storms.

In Amherst, New York, a new solar array is generating electricity for a university but is also generating community, knowledge, and habitat. Our power infrastructure is usually thoroughly out of sight. The sites of production, in particular, are often polluted and dangerous, so the public is kept away. As a result, turning on a light is an act disconnected from its implications; we are not asked to understand the true cost of generating power. By fully integrating a power generation site into the campus, the university has given students an opportunity to comprehend their decisions within a global context. Access empowers, and the paths and landscape rooms within the Solar Strand empower visitors to fully value energy.

On the Gulf Coast, a major enhancement to the storm and flood protection system along Galveston's seacoast is in development. Cities are (relatively) fixed in place, but natural systems are dynamic, creating and eradicating land over time. In coastal regions, those time frames can be quite short when hurricanes strike. A proposal for a new Lone Star Coastal National Recreation Area envisions a recreational and ecological landscape as one defense against storm surges. In addition to a hardened defense infrastructure of gates, dikes, and canals, the National Recreation Area would provide an Olmstedian solution of flood protection first, and recreation and tourism where it can be accomplished "thriftily."

These projects highlight some of the potentials of designing on, with, and like infrastructures. Other infrastructures provide equally complex sites that challenge our creativity, and many are mentioned throughout the pages of this book (see, for example, in other chapters, Jaffa Landfill Park and Northala Fields, considering the waste that results from construction; and the Seymour-Capilano water treatment facility). These projects render visible our cultural relationship with systems—water, power, defense. And they provide opportunities to see and critique our reliance on these invisible systems.

**Verdant surface parking lot for the Venice, Italy, airport expansion, incorporating mature trees, porous pavers, and graphic soil.**

---

**TESSERA, ITALY**

**DESIGNED BY**
MADE associates (Treviso, Italy)

**COMPLETED IN 2011**

**310,000 SQUARE FEET / 28,800 SQUARE METERS**

# MARCO POLO AIRPORT CAR PARK

Airport parking lots generally do not win design awards. They are vast, disorienting, sterile, and on summer days, scorching. A 2011 expansion of the parking lot at Venice's Marco Polo Airport breaks that mold, proposing that parking lots can be locally specific, visually engaging, ecologically productive, and verdant. This project raises airports and car parks to the level of site-specific work rather than treating them as anonymous, in-between landscapes that exist only to link home and a destination.

The parking lot is woven into an existing forest. Trees and a bold path provide clear wayfinding and avoid the numbing loss of place engendered by many parking lots.

---

21

As part of an ambitious twenty-year expansion and development plan for the Marco Polo Airport, MADE associates turned a fallow grove north of the airport terminal into needed parking while integrating the car park into larger landscape processes. The design saved existing mature trees to provide shade and a local identity; other trees were carefully removed and replanted as part of a moveable nursery for the phased expansion. Parking aisles are surfaced with porous pavers to provide the trees with access to air and water and room for root growth. And a vibrant red path meanders through the car park, providing clear wayfinding and a sense of whimsy that is extraordinary in this most banal of landscape types.

Parking is an underconsidered aspect of our urban experience; 30 to 50 percent of the area of U.S. cities is covered with asphalt surface lots, and very few of those are considered as social or ecological spaces. Large lots, such as occur at airports and shopping centers, can be so monotonous and disorienting that visitors lose their way and can't relocate their cars. In a new parking lot for the Marco Polo Airport, the designers have considered this invisible space as a place of arrival and departure, a moment of reorientation for visitors, and a landscape with internal processes. Graphic soil and clumps of trees provide markers in the landscape, serving as wayfinding devices for visitors. The integration of parking into a movable nursery concept is innovative, and the retention of trees and use of porous paving provide models for urban surfaces that can accommodate the needs of people and plants, improve air temperatures and quality, and mitigate flooding.

Unlike adjacent parking lots, the new car park maintains many of the existing trees, a seemingly simple decision that provides a host of benefits.

22

MADE associates provided a landscape master plan for the airport expansion as part of a multinational team. The expansion is part of the Trans-European Transport Network (TEN-T) program, which coordinates and prioritizes transportation infrastructure improvements throughout Europe. (There are additional Trans-European Networks for other infrastructures such as telecommunications.) TEN-T includes all transportation modes—road, rail, air, inland and sea waterways—with specific networks for each. Marco Polo Airport is along a high-speed railway from Lyon to Budapest, one of TEN-T's priority projects, so the airport is being reconsidered as a multimodal hub connecting high-speed rail, local rail, air travel, local transit and roads, and water transport. The ambitious twenty-year expansion plan would create significant commercial and recreational development, including a new "airport city," hotel and conference center, stadium, and large regional park.

MADE prepared a feasibility study of the airport landscape that considered the project as a landscape in time and in motion. The fact that the four-phase development will be carried out over two decades created opportunities for a process-based design where latent areas of the site operate as tree nurseries and material stockpiles. As new phases are constructed, those areas are deconstructed, material stockpiled and reused, and plants relocated to be grown in future development sites. Trees will be used as they are needed from this tree nursery in motion. The project is one of continual recomposition, with soils, surfaces, and trees reused and reconfigured over time.

The new car park was one of the first projects to be realized at the airport. The car park tests the idea of a landscape in motion, through the tree nursery, the paving details, and the design of the walkways. The nursery proposes a landscape literally in motion, as the trees are moved and removed as needed. The paving also literally moves, although at a small scale. Parking stalls are paved with concrete grids through which water can infiltrate and grass can grow, and which can adjust slightly to subsurficial shifts, while black gravel at the trees allows movement of air and water to the tree roots. The walkways also move figuratively; rather than rigid lines laid on the landscape, to which all details are subservient, the walkways are fluid and flexible in their layout. They begin with an intention—to move people from their cars to the central paths to the airport—and then meander around the site's contingencies, its existing trees.

The car park situates 1,200 new parking spaces in an existing wood. The project overlays two distinct geometries: the efficient geometry of drive aisles and parking spots, and the irregular geometry of trees. Drive aisles were cleared, and smaller and understory trees were carefully removed. Select trees that fit into the parking areas were saved, leaving an irregular scattering of about one hundred trees. This allowed approximately 25 percent of the existing tree canopy to remain

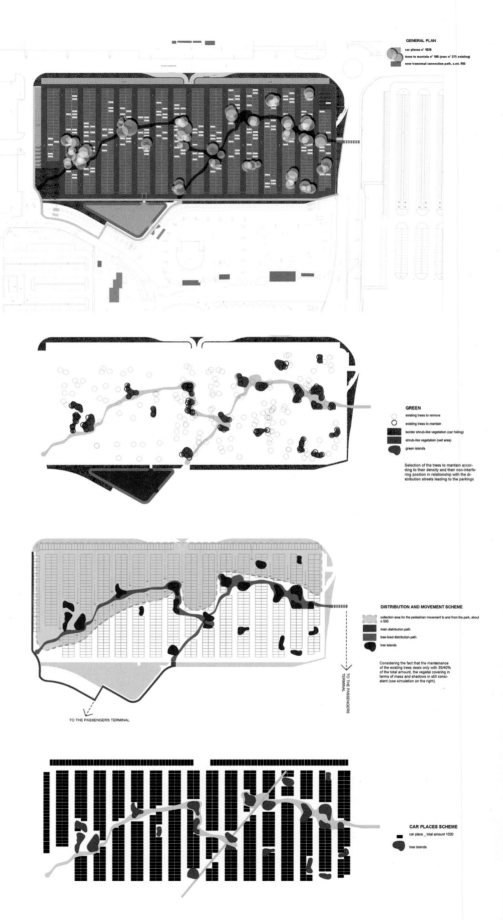

GENERAL PLAN

car places n° 1020
trees to mantain n° 100 (over n° 275 existing)
new traversal connection path, s.mt. 950

The "graphic soil" walkway meanders to create a bold, visually clear path from parking stalls through clumps of trees to existing sidewalks.

The parking lot combines two formal systems: the logic of the parking stall and the existing forest structure.

**24**

INFRASTRUCTURE

GREEN

existing trees to remove
existing trees to mantain
border shrub-like vegetation (car hiding)
shrub-like vegetation (wet area)
green islands

Selection of the trees to mantain according to their density and their non-interfering position in relationship with the distribution streets leading to the parkings

DISTRIBUTION AND MOVEMENT SCHEME

collection area for the pedestrian movement to and from the park, about n 500
main distribution path
tree-lined distribution path
tree islands

Considering the fact that the mantainance of the existing trees deals only with 35/40% of the total amount, the vegetal covering in terms of mass and shadows in still consistent (see simulation on the right).

TO THE PASSENGERS TERMINAL

TO THE PASSENGERS TERMINAL

CAR PLACES SCHEME

car place _ total amount 1020
tree islands

## VEGETATION

1 **Typha minima**
Small inflorescences.
It grows till 75cm - 85 cm.
5 plants in a s.mt. density.

2 **Panicum virgatum 'Northwind'**
Grey, green and blue leaves,
orange during fall.
It grows till maximum 150 cm -
180 cm, 1 plant in a s.mt.

3 **Festuca glauca 'Golden Toupee'**
Yellow-green leaves. It grows
till maximum 20 cm - 25 cm.
9 plants in a s.mt. density.

*Typha minima*

*Panicum virgatum 'Northwind'*

*Festuca glauca 'Golden Toupee'*

while sacrificing about 80 parking spaces (or about 6 percent). Trees removed were planted in meadow areas to mature until they are needed in future designs.

Whereas most of the car parks at Marco Polo are black asphalt, with little (if any) vegetation, the newest one is primarily paved in structured grass. Drive aisles, which need more maintenance and need to be more durable than the parking spots, are paved in asphalt, but the parking spots are precast concrete grid pavers filled with gravel that can support the weight of vehicles but through which grass can grow. This allows the small movements of landscapes: infiltration of water and air to tree roots, and the subtle shifts of ground from growing roots. It also minimizes the heating effect of black asphalt; between the grass pavers and the tree shade, the car park stays substantially cooler than its neighbors.

Airports and parking lots often suffer from monotony and repetition, which can lead to visitor disorientation. In the Marco Polo Airport car park, a series of meandering paths and wooded clumps provide variety within the regular grid of parking spaces, orienting visitors. The regular geometry of cars and the irregular geometry of forests organized the layout of the project and helped to determine

Grasses around the edges were selected for color and seed heads, to help with orientation.

**25**

MARCO POLO AIRPORT CAR PARK

which trees should remain. Once that decision was made, the wooded clumps were connected to major access points along the edges with a meandering path in bright red. Crosswalks are boldly striped for clarity and safety, and each parking aisle along the path is numbered with a vibrant graphic to provide clear wayfinding through the lot. The designers proposed dozens of different versions of the path before striking the right balance: memorable without being overly busy, unified without being monotonous. The solid path, striped crosswalks, and dark gravel tree pits were conceived as graphic soil, a vibrant, sinuous line to clarify and enliven the lot. The bases of the clumps of trees are kept free of paving, enhancing the wooded feeling and providing a clear contrast with the strong graphic design of the paths.

The firm has said of design that "to accompany, to accommodate, to feed growth is to be part of reality—the reality of places, people and emotions—to design places is to write on a living and vital body—to leave upon it a sign, a trace." The car park at the Marco Polo Airport engages that reality and vitality through an innovative infrastructure.

Permeable pavers for the parking stalls allow rainwater to infiltrate to the trees' roots; the growing grass reduces the heat of the lot.

——

Gravel at the trees allows rainwater to infiltrate, while colored concrete provides a durable surface for pedestrians and rolling suitcases.

This view of the graphic soil path shows the bold pattern of the colored concrete and the clear graphic identity of the parking lanes.

**Pedestrian bridge to a historic earthwork fort, using the defensive infrastructure of the past as inspiration to connect the fort to local recreation routes**

———

**HALSTEREN,
THE NETHERLANDS**

**DESIGNED BY**
RO&AD Architects
(Bergen op Zoom, the Netherlands)

**COMPLETED IN 2011**

**540 SQUARE FEET /
50 SQUARE METERS**

# MOSES BRIDGE AT FORT DE ROOVERE

Moses Bridge is an astonishing inversion: a bridge that cuts a dry path *through* the water rather than *over* it, two slivers of wood holding back inundation to allow passage. The bridge is a piece of modern infrastructure inspired by historic infrastructure. The centuries-old fort it accesses was part of an extensive defense infrastructure; the bridge accepts the challenge of boldly sculpting and manipulating water and earth, reminding us that infrastructure need not consist of the usual or the obvious.

A new pedestrian bridge to a historic fort inverts expectations as it passes through a moat.

———

INFRASTRUCTURE

The moat of Fort de Roovere reflects the trees above and the green slopes of the containing embankments. It is a tranquil, smooth line of water, centuries removed from its military origins. But at this park, you are reminded that the moat served a defensive function; the unbroken lines of water and earth held off a siege in 1747. Approaching from the east, the attack side, visitors become aware of a line in the water, which reveals itself from the top of the embankment as a break, a parting of the waters. Incredibly, a path has been carved through the water of the moat. From some angles, heads appear to float through the water and through the depth of the embankment.

Moses Bridge expresses a certain Dutch approach of working within highly engineered natural systems: bold engineering, understanding and respect for the element, and refined artistry. It is a microcosm of Holland and the fort, regulating water and holding it back to create occupiable land. And it is a bewitching and beautiful object that provides a new perspective on the element that, in Holland and other low-lying areas, is simultaneously life-giving and potentially devastating.

In the early seventeenth century, floodable defense lines were built in Holland to protect cities and infrastructure from Spanish attack. The first, the relatively small West Brabant Water Line, ran a little more than 10 miles (16 kilometers), from Bergen op Zoom in the south to Steenbergen in the north. (The Dutch Water Line, in comparison, was 50 miles or 80 kilometers long and 2 to 3 miles or 3 to 5 kilometers wide, with a 125,000-acre or 50,586-hectare inundation zone.) The line was made of a series of earthen ramparts and forts to contain water; an inundation area; and dams, dikes, and locks to control the water level. The northern half could be inundated with salt water from an inlet of the North Sea; the southern half could be flooded with freshwater from a series of natural lakes and ponds. The inundation zone could be flooded to about 15 inches (38 centimeters)—too shallow for enemy boats to float on but deep enough to be impassable for soldiers and vehicles. The line was flooded defensively six times between 1628 and 1830. Fort de Roovere was the largest fort along the West Brabant Water Line, with a moat and outer earthworks surrounding the four-pointed earthwork fort and defending it from attack from the east.

In the nineteenth century, new technology made this extraordinary defensive infrastructure obsolete, and the earthworks and waterworks fell into disrepair. The moat at Fort de Roovere slowly filled in; the earthworks eroded and melted into the surrounding landscape. Beginning in 2010, the group Friends of Fort de Roovere organized renovations to the fort, including removing overgrown vegetation and dredging the moat. The fort is linked to local recreation routes, especially for hiking and biking, and access to the fort was desired. RO&AD Architects was hired to design a bridge to provide an eastern approach over the moat to the upper embankment of the fort.

Historically, the eastern, defensive side had no bridge, but the changed cultural context demanded one. Yet to the design team, it seemed "highly improper to build bridges across the moats of defense works, especially on the side of the fortress the enemy was expected to appear on." So out of respect for the historic integrity of the fort, the design team proposed a bridge through the water rather than over it. Moses Bridge takes its name from the biblical story of the parting of the Red Sea; the bridge audaciously splits the water to reveal a dry path below the water level. But the bridge isn't a miracle; it's a combination of integration and creativity.

The bridge parts the water, creating optical illusions and inversions as it breaks the reflections.

MOSES BRIDGE

Fort de Roovere is part of a landscape-scale defensive infrastructure that used a problem as an opportunity. Located below sea level, much of the country is at risk for inundation. Turning that problem around, seventeenth-century engineers realized that by harnessing flooding, they could manipulate the threshold between dry land and marsh, and could make dry land appear and disappear as needed. Moses Bridge builds on this artistic, ingenious attitude toward water and accepts water—and by extension, project sites—as a sculptable element, not merely a background. And in fact, the bridge is possible through exactly the sort of hydraulic manipulation that created the Water Line. Water does not flow under the bridge; the bridge creates two disconnected pools. Adjustable outflow dams, set to the height of the bridge walls, regulate each pool. In storms, overflow spills over the dams, not into the bridge.

The designers also showed remarkable creativity when they refused to accept anything as absolute. The program called for a bridge. But what was really needed was a connection, a moment within a pedestrian infrastructure. A bridge simply happens to be the most usual infrastructure to connect across water. By recognizing the problems of the usual solution—the insult to the very historic artifact being restored and celebrated—the designers opened themselves to more creative and artistic solutions.

Barely visible at left, the bridge respects the massing of fort and moat.

In the concept sketch, the design is a thin line connecting the two bulwarks.

Moses Bridge is more like earth art than an infrastructural object. This is a perhaps unsurprising closing of a loop; many of the land artists working from the
late 1960s onward looked to the infrastructure of military earthworks, with their
striking geometry and massive manipulations of land, water, and vegetation, as
a source of inspiration and critique. Mary Miss's Field Rotation (1980–81), for
example, is a four-pointed incision into an earth mound that resembles the bas-
tions of forts. It seems fitting to have infrastructure that draws on earth art within
an earth-bermed moat. Moses Bridge recalls Andy Goldsworthy's Storm King
Wall (1997–98), where a stone wall meanders to a stream and apparently dives
below the surface to appear again on the other side, an inaccessible underwater
crossing. More strongly, Moses Bridge echoes Mary Miss's Greenwood Pond:

Double Site (1989–1996) in Des Moines, Iowa. There, as part of a larger art piece, Miss restored a wetland and created a path that provided multiple views of the site—above, along, and within the wetland. In Double Site, the path dives into a concrete room embedded in Greenwood Pond. Wood pylons mark the inaccessible path through the water, which picks up again at a dock across the pond. In the concrete room, visitors can sit and experience the wetland at eye level. The pylons connecting the underwater room and the dock suggest walking through the water; the visitor yearns to complete the journey but is thwarted. In Moses Bridge, the desire to cross through water without getting wet is finally satisfied.

Moses Bridge reminds us that infrastructure need not consist of the usual or the obvious. Infrastructure connects: people, places, material, information. As long as that connectivity is maintained, the infrastructure can take many different forms. At Fort de Roovere, pedestrian infrastructure draws on the physical and cultural history of the site, and operates as installation art. Miss spoke of her work as "questioning the boundaries—physical, spatial, or emotional—that we take for granted." Moses Bridge similarly questions the professional boundaries of engineer, landscape architect, and artist.

Cut into both the earthworks and the water, the bridge is nearly invisible from a distance.

———

Crossing the moat gives a new perspective on the water.

**Urban plaza composed of a small park (Dutch Kills Green), a storm water wetland, and more than a mile of streetscape, bicycle and pedestrian paths, and plantings**

———

**QUEENS, NEW YORK**

**DESIGNED BY**
WRT (Philadelphia), landscape architecture—Margie Ruddick, design lead

Marpillero Pollak Architects (New York City), architecture and urban design

Michael Singer Studio (Wilmington, Vermont), public art

Leni Schwendinger Light Projects (New York City), lighting design

Langan Engineering (New York City), civil engineering

**COMPLETED IN 2012**

**1.5-ACRE PLAZA, 1.3-MILE STREETSCAPE / 0.6-HECTARE PLAZA, 2-KILOMETER STREETSCAPE**

# QUEENS PLAZA

A redesigned streetscape artfully guides and protects pedestrians and creates an urban wetland.

———

Trains squeal overhead on elevated rails. Trucks and cars rush through intersections at a chaotic pace and level of congestion. Through this cacophony, pedestrians and cyclists make their way along a lushly planted green ribbon that provides a safe, well-delineated route. Queens Plaza would be a success for this alone—but it also weaves together transportation, storm water infrastructure, and recreation with ecology and art, creating a hybrid urban place that is part infrastructure, part art, part neighborhood catalyst.

Before reconstruction, the site was a car park, with grassed squares where street trees had died.

Plantings, lane alignments, traffic signals, and artful concrete clarify the site, providing safety and beauty.

INFRASTRUCTURE

Before its reconstruction, Queens Plaza was harsh, hostile, and dangerous. It is the entry to Long Island City and Queens from the Queensboro Bridge, and it was a tangle of elevated and at-grade rail lines and turning, crossing traffic lanes, all navigating the horizontal intersection of gridded street and curving rails, and the vertical exchange from street to bridge. It was, in the words of design website Inhabitat, "well, pretty ugly." And yet the potential for the plaza is significant. It forms the eastern end of an important east-west link, from the southern end of Central Park across the Queensboro Bridge along Queens Plaza to Dutch Kills Green park, and from there, into Long Island City and Queens. It also connects the eastern boroughs to the river, providing important passages within the neighborhood.

The area has easy access to Manhattan, but the snarl of infrastructure and its industrial character made it unattractive for commercial or residential uses. In 2001, seeking to spur development, the city rezoned the area from a mix of industrial uses to high-density, mixed-use commercial and residential. Several infrastructure and open space projects were planned, including Queens Plaza. The project was one of two pilot projects for New York City's High Performance Infrastructure Guidelines and so was intended to test the limits of integrating transportation and storm water infrastructure, ecological function, and social identity and cohesion.

The primary goal of the Queens Plaza redesign was to improve the transportation infrastructure: to smooth the flow of traffic and to provide safe and comfortable bicycle and pedestrian routes. Some areas of the project had as many as sixteen lanes of traffic crossing over multiple intersections, with awkward traffic signaling that led to congestion or vehicles running red lights. The area was dangerous for cars and trucks, but even more so for cyclists and pedestrians. The New York City Department of City Planning and the traffic-engineering firm Eng-Wong, Taub & Associates redirected traffic both temporally, through carefully choreographed traffic signals, and spatially, through spacious planted medians, widened sidewalks, and clear, separated lanes for the various modes of transportation. Improved lighting throughout has also improved safety and comfort. The plaza has been changed, in the words of one bike commuter, from "a horrible 'shooting the rapids' feeling . . . to the much more pleasant and infinitely safer-feeling grade separated and buffered bike route. . . . It went from feeling like the most dangerous part of my route to the safest."

Cuts in the concrete edge allow rainwater to flow from the sidewalk to the rain gardens.

The city wanted to use the project as an example of how transportation infrastructure can do more than simply improve traffic flow. The city's 2005 High Performance Infrastructure Guidelines state, "The manner by which we design, build, maintain, and operate infrastructure within our urban right-of-way profoundly affects our ecology and every measure of our environment. Our natural resources, such as air quality, waterway health, and vegetation, exist in a state of interdependence with each other and with our built urban infrastructure." The guidelines set out a series of performance goals for the public right of way, as a way to reduce both installation and maintenance costs, increase social cohesion and quality of life, and generate environmental benefits such as cooler, cleaner air and water.

Landscape architect Margie Ruddick and architect Linda Pollak designed Queens Plaza to integrate infrastructure, ecology, and art. They worked with artist Michael Singer to design permeable pavers that give a unique character to the district while also allowing storm water infiltration and directing excess storm water to the planting areas. The pavers—interlocking Ls, Ts, and squares—have grooves to direct water; gaps between the pavers allow plants to grow and water to infiltrate to the soil beneath. Nearly five hundred trees were planted in the plaza and streetscape, with a palette of native, drought-tolerant, and noninvasive species adding to the foraging and nesting habitat of the neighborhood.

Water flows to small pockets of planting throughout the streetscape and also to a half-acre wetland in the eastern park. Metal grate walkways draw visitors into the wetland, and benches provide places for people to immerse themselves in the sedges, ferns, and grasses and to observe the birds and butterflies that make a home in this urban fragment. (Perhaps unsurprisingly, the limited flower palette of aster, bur marigold, and swamp dock has been augmented with ruderal species—species that grow on waste ground or refuse—such as purple loosestrife and thistle.) The paving, swales, and wetland reveal the water cycle within the city, clean and cool storm water before excess water enters the storm water system, and irrigate the lush plantings. The system also helps to mitigate flooding as it stores peak storm water, an ecosystem service that has gained value after Hurricane Sandy flooded significant portions of the city in 2012.

In addition to ecological services, the plaza provides economic sustainability by reusing materials and spurring economic development. The concrete from the 73,000 square feet (6,800 square meters) of sidewalks demolished in the project was reused in curbs, median installations, and portions of the wetland. The reused concrete adds to the project's identity and also helps to direct traffic and storm water. The rough edges of the concrete and the serrated, vertical arrangement create protective barriers around pedestrians, and their tough aesthetic stands up to the noise and chaos of the traffic. Few materials would have the visual and

Two views of the same intersection.

Before reconstruction, the tangle of infrastructure was treacherous for pedestrians and cyclists.

After construction, "It went from feeling like the most dangerous part of my route to the safest."

40

physical power to claim a place in this harsh environment, and the concrete is an inspired design that acts as a bodyguard, carving a path for bicyclists and pedestrians through the traffic.

At the eastern end of Queens Plaza, a commuter parking lot was reclaimed as Dutch Kills Green, a 1.5-acre (0.6-hectare) park. Several mature oak trees at the northern end of the park were protected through the construction and provide the preferred seating area in the park. (Not coincidentally, it is also the area farthest from the elevated train lines and therefore slightly less noisy than other parts of the park.) The park provides individual seating and a small amphitheater, and is intended as an urban respite for the neighborhood. While commuters stop briefly and construction workers from an adjacent site rest in the park on breaks, in general the park is not heavily used except as part of a journey. This is primarily a result of the noise; subway trains brake for the overhead curve, and the squeal can surpass a brutal 100 decibels. While Dutch Kills Green is lush and lovely, this is perhaps a lesson to designers to encourage owners to realistically address their sites' potential as an oasis. Queens Plaza, meanwhile, has a large number of visitors in addition to the high volume of cyclists and pedestrians. The benches are popular locations to sit, eat, talk, and people watch, and seem to be particularly popular with high school students.

Queens Plaza has been a notable success. Since it opened, bicycle traffic has increased nearly 25 percent and accidents have decreased. For the first time in recent history, 2011 saw no fatalities on this stretch of road, infamously known as the Boulevard of Death, down from a 1997 high of eighteen fatalities. The path is

The wetlands clean and cool the rainwater and provide a small patch of wild urban habitat.

**42**

INFRASTRUCTURE

shaded and pleasant, and in the wetland, bees and butterflies have made a home there. The greenway connects to the East River, providing a safe route for people and urban animals alike. The park and greenway prevent more than 20 million gallons (76 million liters) of water per year from entering the storm water sewer, a critical benefit in coastal cities such as New York. And between 2006 and 2013, the surrounding properties increased 37 percent in market value.

The plaza shows the importance of integrating landscape architects into the design of our urban infrastructures. While cities may be most interested in the quantifiable benefits of material reuse, storm water reduction, and property value improvement, for residents the less tangible benefits of sociability and quality of life are equally, if not more, significant.

The new bike path is separated from traffic by lush planting and shaded by trees.

QUEENS PLAZA

Solar panel array in a reclaimed
meadow and wetland
ecosystem, incorporating
walkways and outdoor classrooms

———

**UNIVERSITY AT BUFFALO
NORTH CAMPUS, AMHERST,
NEW YORK**

**DESIGNED BY**
Walter Hood (Oakland, California)

**COMPLETED IN 2012**

**6.5 ACRES (4-ACRE SOLAR
ARRAY) / 2.6 HECTARES
(1.6-HECTARE SOLAR ARRAY)**

# SOLAR STRAND

Most solar arrays (like most power generation in general) are
hidden from view. Arrays are often located on leftover land:
on rooftops or beside highways. Or they are fenced off, inaccessible. By making the Solar Strand array highly visible and
accessible, the University at Buffalo has integrated it into the
educational life of the faculty and students, and insinuated the
implications of power generation and use into the conscious-
ness and identity of the university.

A solar array provides
a landscape room
for education and
ecological restoration.

———

The solar array parallels the entry road; the banded forms extend into the landscape and across the road through tree plantings, partially complete in the upper left of this image.

**46**

The entrance to a campus tells you something about its self-identity. Structures, materials, and spatial composition give clues to the university's sense of its place in society. At the University at Buffalo's north campus, visitors enter alongside a solar panel array. This alone signals the university's commitment to research, to sustainability, and to changing social conceptions of power as always invisibly present. But the project tells you more about the university. As the array projects forward into the future, it also reaches back to reclaim history. It is not set in a banal lawn but in a productive ecosystem of meadow and wetland reclaimed from previously drained land. Paths and plazas are made from the physical stuff of the campus, materials reused from demolition projects. And the very accessibility of the power array—the paths through the panels, the plazas created in their shadows—speaks of the university's desire to integrate teaching and learning with technological and ecological productivity. The array parallels the entry road, and the patterns of the array reach across that road in mown paths, meadows, and tree plantings. The patterns form a gateway to campus that foregrounds power as well as sustainability education and research.

The Solar Strand integrates the landscape of power production into the daily life of a community. The strand is informed by, reinforces, and changes the social, educational, cultural, and ecological identity of the university. In most situations, the industrial forms of the array—3,200 3-by-5-foot (0.9-by-1.5-meter) panels—would be placed in a simple, repetitive layout. Instead, Walter Hood used the technological requirements of the array as a design opportunity. The modular panels, their optimal inclination, and the preferred linking of twelve panels to a string and twelve strings to a combiner box created a structure within which Hood improvised to create complexity within simplicity.

The project springs from the University at Buffalo's goal to be climate neutral by 2030. In 2009, the university received a $7.5-million grant from the New York Power Authority (NYPA) to install a solar array to provide power for four housing complexes composed of 735 apartments. The NYPA's goal was maximum power generation, which would normally result in a prosaic, evenly spaced grid. But the university's goals included both power generation and art, education, and research opportunities. It wanted to use the array as a catalyst for education and for changing the public understanding of power use and generation. And it wanted a publicly accessible solar park, one of the largest of its kind in the nation. Through an international design competition, the university sought ideas to frame power generation as land art integrated into the campus landscape. Through an art-based design, the project challenges the segregation of infrastructure and the "not in my backyard" response from communities at the perceived ugliness of the panels, tubes, and grids that provide our power.

Hood's design was inspired by a DNA strand, a biological structure composed of simple elements repeated, recombined to create infinite variety, and also a marker of unique identity. This variety within rigid modularity is a key to creativity when designing infrastructures. The three ribbons of panels—each always twelve panels wide—pattern the landscape by varying the number of panels in a cluster. Based on shadow patterns, shorter sets are tightly clustered and taller sets are spaced farther apart. The shortest are about 4 feet (1.2 meters) tall; their small size humanizes them and provides opportunities for people to explore the panels, to look over them and view them in the landscape. The three tallest—each containing ninety-six panels—create canopies described as "almost cathedral like" by university architect Robert Shibley over landscape rooms that are used as social space, classrooms, or study areas. Knee-height steel tubes containing wires connect the arrays. These frame walkways between the ribbons and also provide physical connection to the array: visitors use them as seats or foot rests. The walkways connect the array to the roads and paths of the campus and create an open work of art: with no clear program to the landscape, visitors are allowed to explore at their own pace and take away what they will from the site. The design, in Hood's

words, "elucidate(s) the idea of energy, of power, and the scale that it takes to generate that power."

But the Solar Strand is more than an accessible power infrastructure. It is also open to the campus, physically, historically, and ecologically. The site originally contained a creek and wet meadow, which were moved and drained for agricultural production. Later, when the campus was developed, the topsoil was stripped, and the area was laid out in the orthogonal forms typical of suburban, car-dependent campuses. The solar array could be a rigid rectangle. But by expanding the linear ribbon forms up to and across Flint Road—the main entrance to the campus—the design has a feathered edge that includes the adjacent creek, vernal pools, and meadow ecosystem. Extensive tree and shrub plantings of maple, catalpa, serviceberry, and witch hazel connect the stream and wetland across the solar array to the marginal tree canopy. The strand was extended beyond the solar array socially as well as physically: more than one hundred students, faculty, and staff helped with tree planting across Flint Road. And the project reclaims the history of the campus's continued development. More than 1,000 tons of brick and concrete from demolition on campus were used to form rubble paths, concrete block seats, and plazas paved in rough concrete slabs.

Grading has begun in this "before" image, showing the degraded ecological condition of the former stream. Past topsoil removal had left thick alluvial clays in which few plants could grow.

INFRASTRUCTURE

The expanded edge is a meadow with walkways defined by mown paths. Where the array produces power, community, and knowledge, the meadow produces soil and habitat. This is the third expanded conception of the site: as a fully productive landscape that combines the engineering of solar technology with the social and ecological technology of landscape architecture. When the topsoil was removed, new alluvium slowly accumulated. Plant growth was difficult in the thick clay, so there were very few trees and shrubs. The meadow of the strand turns the sun's power into a different form of energy: fertile soils. The meadow is constantly changing and regenerating. Native species move in and are cut once a year to reform the site's soils and allow, in the words of Walter Hood, "the simple act of a tree growing."

Native meadows were planted to rebuild fertile soils.

The modular system holds standard-sized panels, connected by conduit that runs close to the ground. The requirements of the solar array created a firm framework within which the designer could innovate.

Larger groups within the array create taller shelters, and because of the shadows they cast, they open up space for large gathering rooms.

Two forms of solar power: the photovoltaic panels generate electricity, while the meadow photosynthesizes to create leaves, flowers, and seeds that will eventually decompose and regenerate the soils.

**50**

The Solar Strand is an optimistic idea, that our infrastructure can be ecologically and socially productive. It embraces contradictions: technology and ecology, energy and soil, rigid structure and playful improvisation. Hood says of the project that its "technology allow(s) us to see ourselves, and to see our place, our smallness in the landscape—but we can control our microclimate, our immediate context." It simultaneously reveals our agency and our limits. The project accepts the constraints of the infrastructure—the modularity, flatness, and repetition—and finds the opportunities within those strictures. But it refuses the usual boundaries of infrastructure: it expands the forms of the array into the ecological and historical context, thereby linking past and future.

The main plaza is paved with reclaimed concrete.

SOLAR STRAND

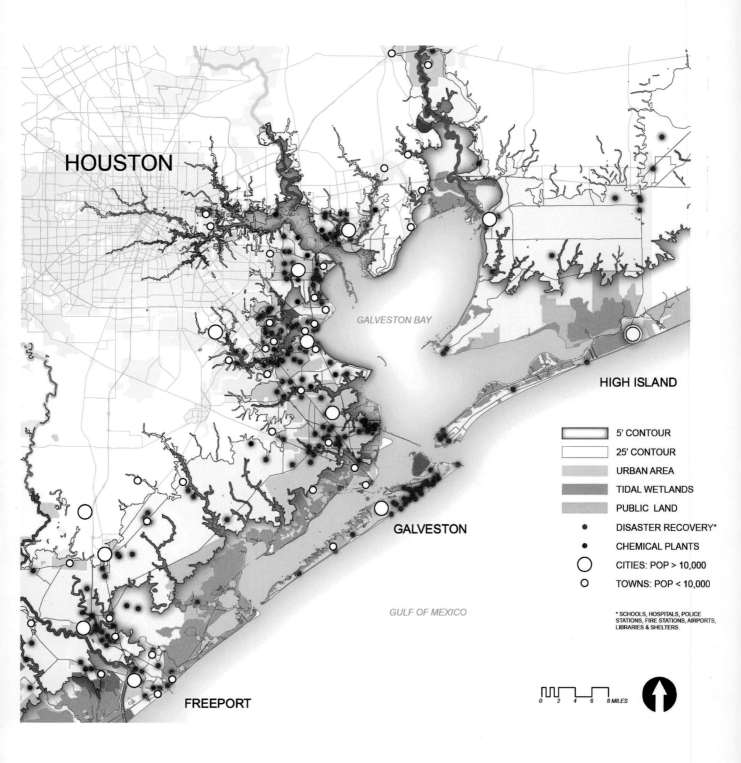

HOUSTON

GALVESTON BAY

HIGH ISLAND

GALVESTON

GULF OF MEXICO

FREEPORT

5' CONTOUR
25' CONTOUR
URBAN AREA
TIDAL WETLANDS
PUBLIC LAND
● DISASTER RECOVERY*
● CHEMICAL PLANTS
○ CITIES: POP > 10,000
○ TOWNS: POP < 10,000

* SCHOOLS, HOSPITALS, POLICE
STATIONS, FIRE STATIONS, AIRPORTS,
LIBRARIES & SHELTERS.

0   2   4   6   8 MILES

**Proposed national recreation area and hurricane protection system including levees, wetlands, and floodgates**

———

**UPPER TEXAS GULF COAST**

**DESIGNED BY**
Professor Thomas Colbert with research assistants Jason Honeycutt and Rose Lee, Gerald D. Hines College of Architecture at the University of Houston

Matt Baumgarten, Alex Lahti, and Fangyi Lu, SWA Group (Houston)

Phil Bedient, Jim Blackburn, and Antonia Sebastian, SSPEED C enter at Rice University

**DESIGNED IN 2012**

**450,000 ACRES /
182,000 HECTARES**

# COASTAL LEVEES AND LONE STAR COASTAL NATIONAL RECREATION AREA

Along Galveston Bay, a large number of urban areas are less than 25 feet above sea level, putting them at risk for floods. A research and design team illustrated the region's vulnerability and proposed both structured and landscape-based defenses.

———

Prone to hurricanes, the Galveston coast is an extremely danger-ous region for development. In large storms, the area is subject to coastal inundation from tidal surges, inland flooding from rainfall, and damage from high winds. Rapid population growth has exac-erbated the risks. After Hurricane Ike in 2008, a multidisciplinary

**INUNDATION**

## 100 YEAR STORM

**19,000**
PEOPLE WITHIN 5' OF SEA LEVEL

**350,000** PEOPLE WITHIN **THE INNUNDATION ZONE**

**48**
CITIES WITHIN 25' OF SEA LEVEL

**22**
CITIES WITHIN 5' OF SEA LEVEL

HOUSTON

BAYTOWN

ANAHUAC

LA PORT

GALVESTON BAY

PEARLAND

CLEAR LAKE

TEXAS CITY

GALVESTON

ANGLETON

GULF OF MEXICO

LAKE JACKSON

FREEPORT

The zone that would be flooded in a major storm contains forty-eight cities and 350,000 people. This map illustrates the flood levels that a 100-year storm would cause and highlights the flood risk of the region.

INFRASTRUCTURE

team of researchers and designers proposed both structural and landscape-based strategies as part of a flood-defense system. The multifaceted approach hybridizes natural and engineered systems. Marshes and meadows store floodwater and dampen storms' intensity, while levees and floodgates provide opportunities for large-scale recreational and ecological systems.

The Severe Storm Prediction, Education, and Evacuation from Disasters (SSPEED) Center, a seven-university consortium of scholars, was established in 2007 to research storm predictions and preparedness on the Gulf Coast and to educate government officials, agencies, and the public on their findings. In September 2008, Hurricane Ike made landfall on the eastern end of Galveston Island and continued north up Galveston Bay, with the center of the storm passing east of Houston. The storm, the third-costliest hurricane in US history, caused $27 billion in damage to the Houston-Galveston coastal region. The widespread damage from the storm highlighted the area's vulnerability to storm surge, flooding, and high winds. Had Hurricane Ike tracked farther west, in more heavily populated and developed areas, the damage could have been much

## LAYERS OF PROTECTION

### PROPOSED LAND USE

+ 25'
PROTECTED
25' CONTOUR

5' TO 25'
WILDLIFE
FARMING
RANCHING

5' CONTOUR

0 TO 5'
NATIONAL RECREATION
AREA STUDY ZONE

HOUSTON
BAYTOWN
ANAHUAC
LA PORTE
PEARLAND
CLEAR LAKE
GALVESTON BAY
TEXAS CITY
GULF OF MEXICO
GALVESTON
ANGLETON
LAKE JACKSON
FREEPORT

▦ HABITAT RESTORATION ZONE

— EXISTING LEVEE

---- PROPOSED LEVEE

0  2  4  6  8 MILES

worse than it was—including greater loss of life as well as toxic spills from damage to the nation's oil industry and processing facilities along the Houston Ship Channel.

After Hurricane Ike, the SSPEED Center was charged with analyzing the impact of Ike, the potential for damage from future storms, and strategies for protecting the Galveston Bay area in the future. The multidisciplinary research team used storm-modeling software and GIS-based analysis of topography, population density, industrial sites, infrastructure, and other criteria to determine the potential for impact from future storms. An area that would be inundated in a 5-foot (1.5-meter) storm surge was rated at high risk, while areas that would become inundated by a 25-foot (7.5-meter) surge were considered at moderate risk. The SSPEED Center research team identified four zones of different landscape character and risk level, and a group of researchers and designers led by SSPEED Center researcher Professor Thomas Colbert of the University of Houston proposed zone-specific strategies for each: Galveston Island, Houston Ship Channel, West Bayshore, and the low-lying coastal areas.

The most vulnerable areas are proposed to be protected by creating a national recreation area and limiting the amount and type of development that could occur.

COASTAL LEVEES

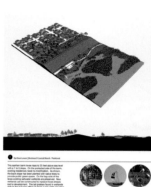

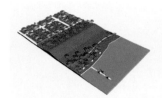

RESTORED MARSHLAND

ELEVATED ARCHITECTURE

RECREATIONAL PIER

ECOTOURISM HOTEL

PROTECTED COMMUNITY

ELEVATED HIGHWAY AND COASTAL MARSH

ELEVATED GALVESTON SEAWALL REDESIGNED PROMENADE

The proposals included a variety of structural and nonstructural flood-control strategies best suited to each zone. The team proposed that the ship channel and Galveston Island—at higher elevations and with high densities of residents, businesses, and industrial sites—would best be protected primarily through structural means (levees and gates). The low-lying coastal areas—with high risk of inundation and lower-density development—could more effectively be protected through landscape-based strategies, and in the mixed-character West Bayshore zone, a hybrid approach was proposed.

The Houston Ship Channel is home to a number of critical oil industry facilities, many of which are only 14 to 16 feet (4.2 to 4.8 meters) above sea level. A severe storm that followed the channel could devastate US oil production as well as create severe toxic spills. To protect the channel from floodwater, the team proposed levees and flood control gates at a narrowed opening to the waterway. Similarly, Galveston Island is extremely vulnerable in spite of a 17-foot (5.2-meter) seawall. The low-lying island has a dense residential and business core on the eastern end. In a severe storm, the island risks complete inundation and becoming inaccessible from the mainland. The team proposed additional levees above the seawall on the bay side of the island, which could also become part of the urban core of the city.

West Bayshore is the district on the western edge of Galveston Bay. The area is vulnerable to flooding; nearly 250,000 residents live within the 25-foot (7.6-meter) storm surge inundation zone. Here, the team proposed a levee system to

The right-of-way for State Highway 146 is proposed as a dike to contain flood-waters along the coast. A range of strategies has been proposed for areas on the inundation side of the highway, from removing structures and restoring wetlands to requiring all new structures to be elevated above flood levels.

In heavily developed areas, where land is constrained, the highway would occupy a seawall.

———

New flood control walls (dashed red lines) are proposed to protect the city of Galveston.

The bay has the highest migratory bird counts in the nation and is ideally suited for kayaking, bird watching, fishing, and hiking.

———

The proposed Lone Star Coastal National Recreation Area protects low-lying areas as natural flood storage.

INFRASTRUCTURE

protect a 25-mile (40-kilometer) stretch of coastal development. While a variety of alignments were considered, the most feasible was a levee incorporating State Highway 146. The highway would be demolished and reconstructed atop the levee. And depending on the landscape context, the levee would provide a wide range of opportunities for ecological restoration and recreation. In higher-density areas, the right-of-way is constrained, and the levee would need to be narrow, a seawall. But in undeveloped or low-density areas, the levees could be gently sloped earth berms with trees planted on the landward side for public open space. In undeveloped areas, the bay side of the levee could be prioritized for wetland protection or restoration—where the marshes help to prevent erosion of the levees—or public parks with access to boating, fishing, and crabbing in the bay. In low-density developed areas, infrastructure on the bay side would need flood protection, and new construction would need to be elevated above the 25-foot (7.6-meter) high-surge line.

On an Army Corps of Engineers boat tour to assess the damage from Hurricane Ike, engineers observed water streaming into the bay from wetlands to the east four days after the hurricane. The wetlands had acted as a sponge, absorbing the 14-foot (4.3-meter) storm surge and releasing the water into the bay over the days following the storm. The fourth protection zone, the low-lying coastal areas, would use the protection offered by the coastal landscape, the tidal marshland, and brackish estuaries, to spread and store floodwater and dissipate the energy of the storm. Undeveloped marshes, coastal prairies, barrier islands, and peninsulas

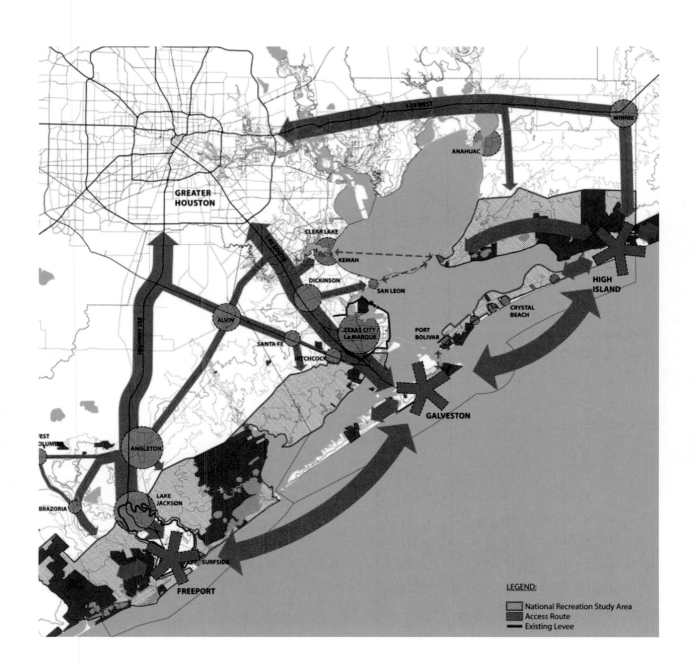

LEGEND:

National Recreation Study Area
Access Route
Existing Levee

along the coast would be assembled into a federally protected buffer against a tidal storm surge. While this would not add storm protection to what already exists, the existing flood storage capacity of the landscape would be protected through the creation of a national recreation area (NRA), a unit within the National Park Service (NPS) system that maintains private ownership and local control of land parcels while coordinating owners and local agencies toward common land use goals. National recreation areas have access to the expertise of the NPS and have a shared identity that is valuable in tourism. Participation is voluntary, an important consideration in Texas where personal property rights are considered inviolable. Consolidating these lands into an NRA would enhance flood protection through marsh preservation and restoration projects while also creating recreation opportunities, economic benefits, and preserved or improved ecosystem function.

The proposed NRA would consist of the coastal inundation zones of four counties. All areas at or below 5 feet (1.5 meters) above sea level—the zone at highest risk for frequent flooding—were considered in the study. Included were approximately 450,000 acres (182,100 hectares) of tidal marshes, brackish estuaries, and coastal prairies, and 150,000 acres (60,700 hectares) of bay. Within those 600,000 acres (242,800 hectares) lie some of the best bird-watching and coastal kayaking areas in the country. While protecting and enhancing the capacity of the landscape to protect urban areas from flooding, an NRA would also provide a significant economic benefit and protect the ecosystem.

A wide range of recreational opportunities exists within the proposed NRA. The islands, estuaries, and forests contain rookeries and other rich areas for bird watching. Galveston Bay is an excellent location for fishing and crabbing, and wildlife areas provide opportunities for seasonal hunting. Bicycle trails could link architectural and historic sites within the district, and the lagoons, inlets, bays, and marshes provide rich opportunities for canoeing and kayaking. By linking existing sites into a coherent destination offering natural richness and beauty, local communities could protect their ecosystems, protect the coast from hurricanes, and bring in significant tourist revenue. An economic impact study estimates that after ten years, the NRA could generate 1.5 million visitors and nearly $200 million in local sales, as well as increase jobs in tourism by 11 percent.

The Galveston Bay evacuation zone is currently home to 1.5 million people, and that population is projected to rise to 2.4 million by 2035. Experts estimate that the existing infrastructure has the capacity to evacuate 1 million people in thirty-six hours, falling far short of accommodating the predicted population growth. And those estimates are for existing landscape conditions. Low estimates for climate-change-based sea level rise in the area over the next century predict an increase of about 2.3 feet (0.69 meters); high-range estimates predict about 4.9 feet (1.5 meters). Even without a hurricane, that much increase in sea level would displace between 78 and 93 percent of households in Galveston County.

Galveston Bay is just one of thousands of such at-risk coastal regions. Landscape-scale planning is necessary to respond to the clear threat of flooding. The proposals for Galveston Bay provide an innovative model suggesting structural, landscape-based, and hybrid approaches to making communities more resilient to rising sea levels and storm surges. The design process is also a valuable model of a research-based consortium analyzing natural disaster risk. Legitimate proposals for resilient communities need to be situated at the intersection of complex ecological, infrastructural, political, economic, and climatological research. The SSPEED Center team used storm-modeling software and GIS-based analysis to evaluate risk and identify innovative opportunities to use resiliency in the face of that risk as a generator of social, economic, and ecological benefits.

The proposed recreation area would have boat launches and viewing platforms for watching birds as well as the enormous ships making their way to the Houston Ship Channel.

COASTAL LEVEES

# POSTINDUSTRIAL LANDSCAPES

## Reclaiming Sites of Industry

Paddington Reservoir
Gardens in Sydney,
Australia.

**DESCRIBING HIS WORK** at Duisburg-Nord Landscape Park, a former steel mill, Peter Latz called it "'design' by handling the existing"—a design practice that begins with site analysis, that sets aside aesthetic prejudices and sees the site simply, diachronically, as it is. Elizabeth Meyer has written on the concept of a figured ground, a way of perceiving sites as always already occupied by landscape structures such as geology and hydrology. Her construct recognizes that sites are not neutral fields awaiting design; they are occupied. The recent design of postindustrial sites has been heavily influenced by these two constructs—one calling for recognition of the preexisting site, the other describing an opportunistic and strategic way of designing with the leftover land resulting from abandoned or obsolete infrastructures.

As populations urbanize, we have two options for accommodating them: increase the physical space of cities or increase their densities. Lacking greenfield sites, or wanting to protect them, cities have turned to reclaiming sites previously used by industry. Many of these sites were developed for industrial use in the early twentieth century and were on the periphery of the city at the time. Cities have grown around them, rendering them less useful for industrial purposes. Often these sites have excellent access to infrastructure, including urban waterfronts.

The postindustrial landscape can be many things: dangerous and toxic; experimental; a repository of cultural memory and identity; a statement of future goals. Postindustrial sites are often loci of civic pride (in past productivity) and identity; they are often in blue-collar neighborhoods and provide potential land banks for market-rate and affordable housing. However, they are often contaminated, making them expensive to clean and raising issues of environmental justice. Postindustrial sites are filled with the physical and environmental legacy of the Industrial Revolution. They are sites of extraction, transport, processing, and waste; mines, factories, rail yards, and landfills are among the wasted sites of obsolete or exported practices.

Rich Haag's Gas Works Park (completed in 1975) in Seattle was among the first landscape architectural projects to retain the artifacts of industry as part of a design. Haag and others, notably Peter Latz at Duisburg-Nord Landscape Park (completed in 1991), evidence a twentieth-century "industrial sublime" aesthetic, engaging the vastness, the awe, and the horror of abandoned factories and rail yards. The scale of many of these sites is monstrous. The projects are also influenced by the depictions of machinery and factories by painters such as Charles Sheeler, the use of industrial materials by sculptors such as Eva Hesse, and the land art of Robert Smithson and others. Smithson famously said, "I'm interested in collaborating with entropy." His work engaged the change and disordering of sites over time, often at the geologic timescale; that inquiry informs much current practice on postindustrial sites, which seeks to reveal the entropy of a site by retaining artifacts and aestheticizing the rust and the ruin.

Postindustrial sites often have complicated histories of productivity. The original greenfield site had an ecological structure that may reemerge in ruderal plants, and depending on the past use, there may be exotic species thriving in nonnative environments. The industrial use may have left physical traces in infrastructures, buildings, and soils, some of which may be dangerous. And depending on the time of industrial abandonment, there may be a history of site use, sanctioned or otherwise, after the industry left. Peter Eisenman's writings on the site as a palimpsest have proven a useful frame for postindustrial sites, considering sites as "deeply scored" by layers of past histories.

At Paddington Reservoir Gardens in Sydney, Australia, the deep scores of a multivalent history are revealed in the design of a collapsed Victorian-era water reservoir. The site had been through many incarnations: a reservoir, a gas station, a parking garage, a neighborhood park, and an abandoned site of unsanctioned occupation. The skillful design of the new park weaves all these histories into a unified site that reveals the palimpsest of cultural occupation.

Jaffa Landfill Park in Tel Aviv, Israel, tells a more limited story but one with deep social and political resonance. The site has a painful and contested history. The seaside slope was a beach for the largely Arab town of Jaffa and was turned into a municipal landfill after the city was incorporated into Tel Aviv. The landfill held the demolition rubble from destroyed Arab houses and eventually became so high that it blocked the view of the sea from portions of Jaffa. The park reclaims those views and tells some of that difficult history as a form of healing garden, bearing witness to the conflict and damage of the site. Here, one history is so powerful that the notion of a palimpsest is less useful; the site speaks with multiple voices but tells different views of a single story.

At the Salvation Army Kroc Center of Philadelphia, the factory history of the site is largely suppressed. Instead, the project reaches further back, to the ecological potential of the region. The factory had left a large volume of heavily contaminated soils, some of which had to be removed off-site while others were allowed to remain, provided they were deeply buried. This remediation process structured the site, as it required a Herculean excavation campaign. The site's balanced cut and fill results in an undulating topography that creates lawns, hills, and marshes. The remediation process allows a design strategy that leaps into the past before the industrial history, to an ecological prehistory.

Rather than choosing to present either cultural or natural history, the Haute Deûle River Banks sustainable district in Lille, France, hybridizes them. The site was once occupied by a textile mill built on a drained marsh. The current redevelopment restores the ecological function of the destroyed marshes through canals and a water garden that cleans and cools rainwater before releasing it to the adjacent Deûle River. The water garden provides a foreground to the historic mill building and resembles a piece of cloth woven with a warp of water and a weft of paths. Site materials reference the industrial past and reveal both the cultural and ecological productivity of this landscape.

West of London, four round hills rise at Northala Fields Park. The mounds are formed on clean fill from construction and demolition projects around the region. Here, the site itself doesn't contain an industrial history, but it has imported the remnants of industrial processes. The park uses the physical remains of material processes as its signal feature, and in the process, it funded its own construction through tipping fees. The project presents postindustrial sites not as something to erase or manage but as an ongoing productive resource still engaged, even in their decline, in cultural production.

Postindustrial sites are rich in possibility. While they often have vexing issues, like the contamination at the Kroc Center, they also have material, cultural, and ecological resources that can be used in locally specific designs that celebrate a region's past, not nostalgically or naively but honestly. Hargreaves Associates, in designing the landfill-turned-park Byxbee Park (completed in 1991) for the city of Palo Alto, California, organized the site conceptually through cultural resources, including Native American artifacts; natural resources, of the bay marshes, sea birds, and wind; and "unnatural resources" of the landfill's own processes of decomposition, methane production, and leachate. This honest analysis of the site provided unique and haunting design opportunities at the park. As we continue to seek new sites in cities, we will continue to be challenged by the toxic, the ugly, the dangerous. The projects in this chapter provide models of highlighting industrial history, ameliorating it, and hybridizing it with other histories. Looking at these sites unflinchingly requires honesty and courage, but it reveals new design strategies, new forms, and often, cultural histories that empower communities.

Reconstruction of a
neighborhood park—including a
roof deck lawn, a sunken garden,
and a reservoir chamber—in
a decommissioned reservoir

———

SYDNEY, AUSTRALIA

DESIGNED BY
JMD Design (Redfern, New South
Wales), landscape architects

Tonkin Zulaikha Greer (Sydney),
architects

COMPLETED IN 2009

12.43 ACRES / 5 HECTARES

# PADDINGTON RESERVOIR GARDENS

At Paddington Reservoir Gardens, decommissioned industrial
infrastructure becomes an opportunity for a reflection on authen-
ticity. The materials and forms of history are presented and
represented, while the climate is acknowledged and ameliorated
to provide the neighborhood with a park that performs both pro-
grammatically and socially. The park combines aspects of sunken
plazas, the romance of industrial ruins, and green roof technology.
These three elements balance each other, providing urban refuge,
rootedness, and continuity.

A new park in an old
reservoir presents a
palimpsest of the site.

———

**69**

The roof of a decommissioned underground reservoir in the Paddington neighborhood of Sydney had been used for years as a neighborhood park. When sections of the roof collapsed in 1991 and the city closed the structure, the neighborhood needed new open space. The reconstructed reservoir, designed by JMD Design (landscape architects) and Tonkin Zulaikha Greer (architects), provides a new type of urban park for Sydney. The designers used the existing conditions of the site to create a complex urban section that acknowledges the roles of history, climate, and social context in shaping cities. In rethinking decommissioned infrastructure, they minimized material use, reduced construction costs, and created a unique local park.

The original intention for the park was to recreate the lawn that had been there before the roof collapsed. The reservoir was built in the late nineteenth century (two chambers opened in 1866 and 1878) and was decommissioned in 1899 as the city grew beyond the capacity of its water infrastructure. After use as a garage and service station, the upper level was grassed over and used as a park, while the lower level was used as a parking garage. When portions of the roof collapsed, the garage and park were closed, and the city looked for ways to stabilize the structure and reopen a park. The forms, light quality, and materials of the reservoir inspired the designers to propose something more than a replacement lawn. They were also inspired by the visible layers of history in the reservoir, graffiti inside the chamber, and the potential for the new design to enter into a dialogue with those layers.

The park has a sunken garden at center, flanked by a rooftop lawn over the existing reservoir chamber, and a seating area at the road. The areas, seemingly contiguous in the plan, are revealed as quite distinct in the section.

Reusing portions of the reservoir provides a variety of microclimates: enclosed, buffered, exposed.

———

This early watercolor sketch highlights the way the physical remove of the sunken garden creates a calm, dreamlike environment for contemplating the passage of time.

POSTINDUSTRIAL LANDSCAPES

OATLEY ROAD

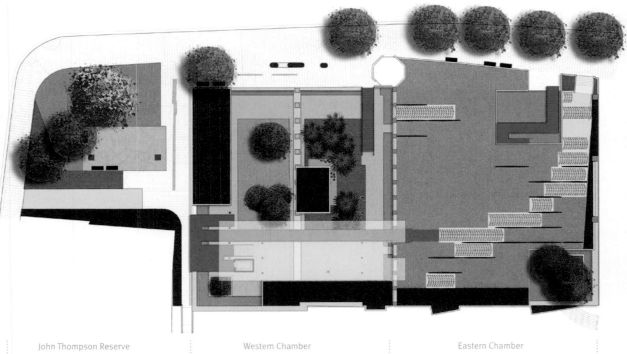

| Oatley Road | John Thompson Reserve | Western Chamber | Eastern Chamber |

The abandoned site showed traces of its history: the vaulting of the Victorian reservoir, a ramp from its use as a garage, and graffitti from its derelict phase.

Placing a park below grade goes against conventional wisdom that a disconnected park will not be successful. Sunken plazas of the mid–twentieth century were often criticized for a perceived lack of safety; with too few points of access and too few eyes on the plaza, visitors felt trapped and unprotected, while the same lack of oversight emboldened some users to engage in illicit activity (such as the graffiti at the Paddington reservoir). But at Paddington, the thoughtful use of the existing structures, the variety of spaces at both street level and sunken level, the variety of sightlines into the park, the ample and dynamic lighting, and the selected closing of portions or all of the park at certain hours combine to create a park that is well used and as a result feels safe. Beyond that, it creates an otherworldly place within the city, a place apart that draws users to its calm remove.

The romance of ruins is no innovation: from the garden follies at Stourhead in Wilshire, England, to Gas Works Park in Seattle and more contemporary examples, landscape architecture has long drawn on ruins as a means of connecting people to history and to place. Artists from Piranesi to Charles Sheeler and Robert Smithson drew attention to both the beauty and the sublime quality of industrial structures. Increasingly, cities and private agencies are embracing this aesthetic as a means of both expressing history and reusing existing infrastructure. Paddington Reservoir Gardens connect the site to its neighborhood by revealing multiple histories. The Victorian era is revealed in the reservoir itself—the brick arches and vaulted chambers—and represented in the fern garden, reminiscent of Victorian fern rooms. The era of the neighborhood park and service station is recreated in bright red benches located where the former pumps stood. The era of decline is revealed in the graffiti left on the old columns, not portrayed as naïf art but simply as another way the neighborhood occupied the site. And the current era is shown in the crisp metal stairs and canopies, the concrete and grass layered on the reservoir roof, and the contemporary lighting.

While the use of history connects the park to its neighborhood, the strategy of sectional inversion creates a sense of remove. Sections of the park are either lifted slightly above or sunken well below street level, giving the visitor an opportunity for overlook or introversion, apart from the neighborhood. And in the lower level, the plants, water, and shade combine to create a microclimate that is significantly cooler than the hot Sydney summer. Shade prevents materials from absorbing solar heat; plants breathing and water evaporating cool the temperature just a bit more. In the heat of the city, the park's microclimate creates a pocket removed from the neighborhood.

The upper level of the park, while physically supported on the eastern reservoir chamber, is organized around representations of history. The grass field is slightly raised above street level. It is reached either by short stairs or by a long catwalk ramp that runs dramatically above the eastern gardens. The structure of the vaults below organizes the lawn: concrete walkways reflect the form of the vaults and contain salvaged brick and steel; and where portions of the roof collapsed, trees were planted below to eventually emerge above the lawn. New pergolas also use the module of the vault and are made of perforated metal that reflects the brick module of the reservoir. A streetside fountain reminds visitors of the original water infrastructure of the reservoir, and red benches along the street reflect the shape, location, and color of the former gas pumps.

History is the subject of the lower level as well, but here it is presented more than represented. Walls, arches, and vaults have been carefully edited and stabilized to

Preserving history: remaining columns and arcades were used as the framework for pavilions and walkways.

73

create the organizing structure of the sunken gardens. The majority of the roof was removed on the eastern portion, and the lower level, formerly full of water, is now filled with a frangipani garden and a tree fern garden, divided by a line of original brick arches. Small portions of vaulting remain on the line of arches and on the western edge; these have been stabilized with concrete and covered with inaccessible aerial planters at street level. The eastern chamber is rarely accessible to the public, but when it is, it is revealed as a brick vaulted hypostyle hall with dramatic colored lighting and historic graffiti.

History is also represented in the sunken gardens, although in ways that make the insertions distinct from the presented historic elements. A pond reminds the visitor of the water that filled the reservoir, although the pond carefully avoids touching the original columns that it surrounds. The tree fern garden reflects Victorian

Representing history:
a new walkway hovers
through the air, connect-
ing the street and lawn.

tastes, and elevated boardwalks around the edges use the meter of the vault. Here, representations of history skirt and skim actual history, and the visitor is held slightly apart from the historic objects.

If history serves to connect the garden to its community, section and microclimate serve to disconnect it from context. The slight rise to the upper level creates a gentle hill, elevated above the neighborhood. And more significantly, the descent to the lower level removes visitors to a site outside of daily urban context. Noise is reduced; sightlines are limited. The gardens are an urban reserve. And the shade provided by roof remnants and walkways creates cool relief from the Australian sun. By negotiating connection and remove, the designers have created a unique park rooted in its history and climate.

PADDINGTON RESERVOIR GARDENS

Reclamation of a landfill into
a regional park including beach,
promenade, amphitheater,
open space, and garden

———

**TEL AVIV, ISRAEL**

**DESIGNED BY**
Braudo-Maoz Landscape
Architecture Ltd. (Tel Aviv, Israel)

**COMPLETED IN 2010**

**50 ACRES / 20 HECTARES**

# JAFFA
# LANDFILL PARK

Removing a landfill
reconnected the city
to the sea and provides
common ground
for a community.

———

Jaffa Landfill Park is built on a site where physical and social histories have intertwined for centuries. Braudo-Maoz Landscape Architecture used the removal of a landfill and reconstruction of a seashore to ameliorate a painful past and serve as a springboard for social discourse. The project removes the physical trace of a contested period in Jaffa's history and reestablishes visual, climatic, and physical connections to the sea that reaffirm the identity of the city. The park is the largest recycling project Israel

By the 1970s, 50-foot (15-meter) cliffs of rubble, largely from demolished Arab neighborhoods, separated Jaffa from the sea.

The new topography of the park allows views to the sea and lets sea breezes into the city. A 1,300-foot (400-meter) sand beach provides access to the sea for swimming and sunbathing.

**78**

has undertaken: more than 1 million tons of material were sorted, crushed, and reused on-site and in other local projects.

Jaffa, south of Tel Aviv, has been a thriving port for millennia. It is the mythical site of Perseus's rescue of Andromeda, and Jonah's ill-fated embarkation for Tarshish. In the early twentieth century, Jaffa was a wealthy district primarily inhabited by Muslim Arabs, although the city has historically had a mix of Arab, Jewish, and Christian residents. After 1948—the War of Independence or the Nakba (catastrophe), depending on perspective—most wealthy Arabs fled Jaffa, which was incorporated into Tel Aviv in 1950. The seaside slope of Jaffa was used as a municipal landfill and eventually held 1.3 million tons of construction and demolition rubble, a large portion of which was generated by the demolition of vacant Arab homes. Members of the Arab community sued to stop the dumping in the 1980s. By then, the "garbage mountain" was 50 feet (15 meters) high, was occupied by herds of goats and criminals, and blocked Jaffa's views of the sea as well as its sea breezes. Illegal dumping continued in the landfill, and the site was an environmental hazard, contributing to air and water pollution, and prone to spontaneous fires.

With environmental concerns as a catalyst, the city of Tel Aviv–Jaffa approved a master plan for the shoreline in 2003. The plan called for stitching together existing beaches and promenades with new infrastructure to create a continuous network of passive and active recreation. The new seashore park is part of an 8.5-mile (13.7-kilometer) network connecting the Tel Aviv seashore from Herzliya (approximately 5 miles or 8 kilometers north of central Tel Aviv) to Bat Yam (approximately 2.5 miles or 4 kilometers south), linking a variety of neighborhoods and suburbs to each other and the sea. The park provides recreation opportunities

A slope to the park blooms in native wildflowers.

**79**

JAFFA LANDFILL PARK

The park heals a wound without concealing its marks. It reclaims a sea-shore that was taken from the neighborhood and tells a new story about the city.

Paving at the overlook includes tiles reclaimed from the rubble, which included homes from predominantly Arab neighborhoods.

for the neighborhood as well as connections through a promenade to the larger park system. A meandering boardwalk traverses protective riprap to the north and buffered beach to the south and divides the sea from planted areas of hills, playgrounds, and recreation fields. Three allees stitch the park to the neighborhood, providing shaded access to the shore.

Public participation was important in defining the project, both in determining the program and in designing the process of reclamation. To connect Jaffa both physically and visually to the sea, the garbage mountain that had been built over thirty years had to be removed. Continuous dumping had moved the shoreline as much as 650 feet (200 meters) into the sea in some locations, and the local sandy beaches had been obliterated. Initial estimates determined that 120,000 truckloads of material would need to be removed. Residents were concerned about the impact that would have—the noise, dust, and traffic of eighteen months of continuous excavation. As a result, every attempt was made to reuse material on-site. Equipment was brought in for material sorting and grinding. In the end, 30,000 truckloads were removed from the site, a 75-percent reduction in traffic from initial estimates. In addition to minimizing the neighborhood impact, the material reuse reduced the cost of the project by nearly 70 percent and also provided less-measurable benefits in terms of reduced vehicle miles and reduced embedded energy costs that new materials would have had.

The site created planting challenges for the park, which is intended as an urban showpiece. During the construction process, in fall 2008, the city of Tel Aviv experienced record water shortages after four consecutive dry winters and placed a ban on planting lawns and decorative gardens. The Jaffa Landfill Park was nearing completion but planting the lawn areas was not allowed, and as a result, the slopes were dusty or muddy, depending on the weather, and eroding. Eventually the important park received permission from the city for planting; the slopes were planted with salt- and drought-tolerant grasses and irrigated with desalinated seawater. Soils were reused, or even manufactured, on-site, and there was some

A new sand beach was constructed from recycled material. A path indicates the historic shoreline. Signage will eventually tell the story of the mutable shoreline.

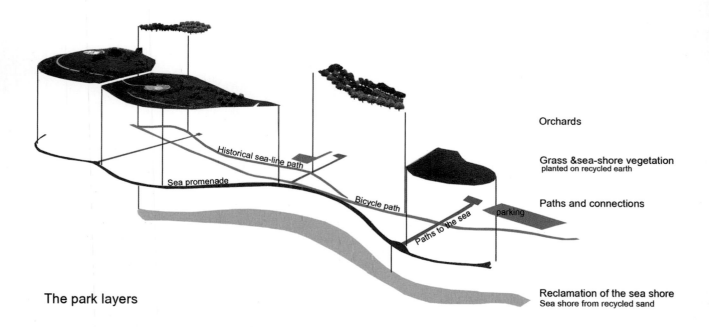

**The park layers**

Orchards

Grass &sea-shore vegetation
planted on recycled earth

Paths and connections

Reclamation of the sea shore
Sea shore from recycled sand

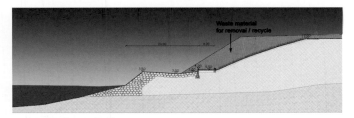

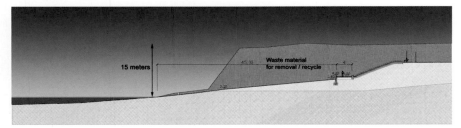

concern about the viability of the soil. During construction, a test garden was planted with more than a thousand trees, shrubs, and ground covers to study the quality of the recycled soils, which were found to be suitable for the park.

The Jaffa Landfill Park has a cautious relationship with history, gently referencing the past through design elements. One of the paths marks the historic shoreline, but there is no reference to why the shoreline has moved; the history of demolition and infill along the coast is silent. Similarly, paving at the crest of the hill contains tiles reclaimed from the landfill, remnants from the homes that were destroyed. These materials hint at the processes of dwelling, abandonment, destruction, and reclamation that have shaped this park. While some critics feel that by erasing a reminder of past wrongs the project denies those events, others feel that the act of reconnecting city and sea is an important physical metaphor for social coping. Perhaps the history is too fresh, still unfolding, and these moments provide opportunities for reflection and personal insertion into the site's history.

The park negotiates its physical and social context to renew connections between communities and sites. The site's difficult social history is barely hinted at in the design, and yet the removal of an offending imposition, the reuse of materials to build healthy ground, and the reconstruction of lost landscapes all provide common ground that is simultaneously a huge public works project and a small but firm ameliorative gesture.

To create the park, 1.2 million tons of waste were excavated, sorted, and crushed. A third of this was used on-site as soil, sand, and base material for paths. The remainder was sold to other sites for use as path and roadbed material.

———

A viewing platform intersects the riprap shore, extending the walkway out to the sea.

**Reclamation of a factory brownfield into a community center that includes sports fields, a playground, formal gardens, an urban farm, and filtration swales**

———

**PHILADELPHIA, PENNSYLVANIA**

**DESIGNED BY**
Andropogon Associates, Ltd. (Philadelphia), landscape architects

MGA Partners, Architects (Philadelphia), architects

**COMPLETED IN 2010**

**12.43 ACRES / 5 HECTARES**

# SALVATION ARMY KROC CENTER OF PHILADEPHIA

The Kroc Center of Philadelphia reintegrates a former industrial site into its economic, ecological, environmental, and social systems. Through creative material reuse, the site sculpts storm water into swales and rain gardens, creating lawns and gardens for visitors, and patches of bird and insect habitat in an urban district. Throughout the design, the industrial history of the site is treated not as the cause of problems to be fixed but as a source of both constraints and opportunities for innovative design.

On a once-toxic site, paths, lawns, gardens, and fields provide places for games and relaxation in the neighborhood.

———

The new design uses soil remediation as a design strategy, creating berms and swales that organize the outdoor rooms and create habitat patches for birds and insects.

———

The 12.5-acre (5-hectare) site was largely paved over, and soils were contaminated from years of use as a train car factory.

In northern Philadelphia, vacant industrial lands are not uncommon. As in many American cities, small industries have been merged into larger corporations, and industrial manufacturing has moved to areas of the world where labor is relatively inexpensive. After the Budd Company car and rail body factory in Philadelphia's Nicetown neighborhood closed in 2002, the 12.5-acre (5 hectare) site was used as a city car impoundment lot. Slag from manufacturing had contaminated much of the soil, and 75 percent of the site was paved. But in designing the site for a new community center, Philadelphia-based Andropogon Associates, experts in ecological and storm water design, conceived of the site as living and connected, rather than toxic, off-limits, and disconnected.

The new Salvation Army community center building provides a gym, swimming pools, and meeting spaces for the community, and the site provides recreation, social, and gardening areas. The site centers on a gently sloping multiuse lawn, which acts as a gathering and performance space. Curving around this lawn, four rain gardens buffer the gathering space from active recreation areas, including sports fields, a playground, and a community garden. Formal gardens mark the passage from site to building, and street plantings create a porous boundary with the neighborhood.

The surrounding area is largely industrial, with residential neighborhoods to the south. Train tracks create strong borders at the southeast and southwest, as does a busy road to the northeast. While pedestrian access is accommodated, current access is largely by car and bike. It is hoped that the community center will act

as a catalyst for redevelopment in this neighborhood, although that has yet to happen. The community center creates the potential for a courtyard to the north, should two factory and warehouse buildings be redeveloped in the future. When that happens, bike and pedestrian paths can easily connect this north lot to the community center.

The Kroc Center uses its industrial history as context: the past is a moment in time that creates problems and challenges the designers' creativity. On this site from 1915 to 2002, the Budd Company manufactured automobile bodies, wire-spoked wheels, and train and subway car bodies, and it contributed to the war effort during both world wars and the Korean War. Nearly ten thousand men and women were employed at the site during its years of peak operation. The company moved its headquarters to Troy, Michigan, in 1972, and began closing plants

around the country. The Philadelphia plant was closed in 2002 as the company consolidated operations in Michigan.

During the site's use as a factory, stockpiled materials and industrial processes contaminated portions of the soil with benzopyrene and heavy metals. The best remediation technique for the stable contaminants was deep burial, although regulations required that some soils be removed off-site. The designers used the constraints of the earthworks—extensive cut and fill that would properly sequester the soils while protecting groundwater—to divide the site into program spaces. Swales and berms divide and buffer the lawn, formal garden, parking lot, playing fields, and urban farm from each other and the busy streets.

Three processes, each with its own goals and imperatives, organize the site—topography, habitat, and water. The topographic design removes and reuses acres of asphalt, removes or sequesters contaminated soils and protects the groundwater, provides level places for recreation, and buffers outdoor rooms from noise and pollution. The ecological design creates a diversity of ecotypes and microclimates, providing a wide range of nesting and foraging opportunities for birds, insects, and small mammals. And the water design minimizes flood potential through storm water storage, cleans and cools runoff, infiltrates water to the water table, and provides spatial division, animation, and a water source for animals. These varied processes and patterns are resolved in the design through an organizing spine of earth berms and rain gardens that divide active and passive recreation zones.

Cleaning up the toxins was obviously the primary site design concern, and the constraint of excavating contaminated soils provided an unusual topographic design opportunity. Seeking to minimize material waste and costs, Andropogon balanced cut and fill with a sinuous grading design. Preliminary calculations showed a balance of cut and fill, but it became apparent during the construction

Asphalt on-site was crushed and reused, and the entire site regraded to remediate the contaminated soils.

POSTINDUSTRIAL LANDSCAPES

document phase that there was an excess of soil on-site. The designers regraded the site, adding 8 inches (20 centimeters) evenly, and in doing so, saved the client $300,000 in hauling and tipping fees. This engagement with material processes also informed the design approach to the existing parking lots. The designers strove for a zero-waste design. Approximately 12,000 cubic yards (9,175 cubic meters) of asphalt and concrete paving, gravel sub-base, and abandoned railroad ballast were reused as rough fill and sub-base for the site. The resulting berms and hollows sculpt rooms from the site and provide channels for water to flow, acting as thresholds between districts.

Throughout the design, the design team sought to provide healthy habitat for people and other creatures, and the topography provides a framework for ecological diversity. Berms and swales offer a diversity of microclimates suited to different ecotypes. To provide bird, insect, and small mammal habitat, different zones of the site were planted in native plant communities, including lowland, upland, and wetland plant associations. The plants provide food and nesting opportunities for native animals and insects, and a resting point for migratory species. The design team continues to monitor the site on a pro-bono basis to ensure that nonnative species are weeded out and that the plant communities are receiving proper maintenance during the establishment phase. The design also includes a ⅓-acre (0.13-hectare) urban farm with an adjacent outdoor classroom. The farm, which opened in spring 2013, provides both produce and knowledge to the families who use the center.

The need to excavate some soils led to a topographic design that guides storm water and organizes the site. A line of rainwater ponds separates active and passive recreation areas.

By balancing cut and fill, the designers sculpted the earth into outdoor rooms buffered from traffic noises and also saved considerable construction costs through avoided tipping fees.

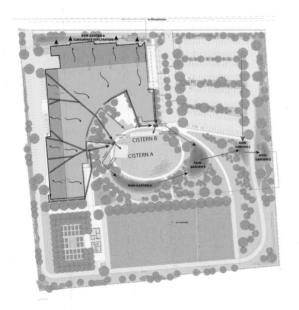

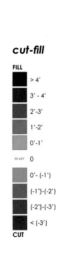

cut-fill

FILL

> 4'

3' - 4'

2'-3'

1'-2'

0'-1'

50'x50'    0

0'- (-1')

(-1')-(-2')

(-2')-(-3')

< (-3')

CUT

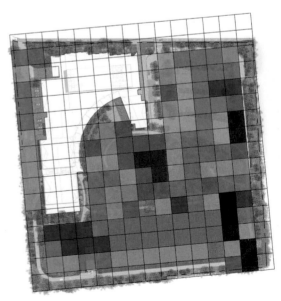

Edges are buffered with meadows and shrubs, which filter views, noise, and pollution and also provide habitat for birds and insects.

Rainwater and air conditioning condensate are guided through granite runnels to cisterns. The water is a clear presence on the site, organizing the landscape rooms.

Rainwater is gathered for reuse in two underground cisterns. Excess flows through a series of rain gardens before overflowing to the city storm water system. The gardens slow, cool, and clean the rainwater, and allow it to infiltrate into the groundwater table.

**90**

The water cycle is the third process organizing the site. Four rain gardens gather runoff from the building and site, including the parking lot. As water moves through the wetland plants, debris is removed, the water is cooled and cleaned, and the water infiltrates down to the water table. A fifth rain garden along Wissahickon Avenue collects more-contaminated runoff from both the building and the street. This linear swale is lined; water is cleaned and cooled but not allowed to infiltrate. Water from the air conditioning system is captured and stored in a cistern for use in irrigation. This water is displayed on the site through granite runnels that provide sound and movement during the summer months.

The Kroc Center is a model being built around the country, a town center for underserved neighborhoods. As such, it is connected to the social habitat structure of the city, providing space for recreation, religious observation, community meetings, and other activities that help build community. Its industrial history created vexing conditions for the designers—acres of asphalt, and contaminated soils—that were reconsidered as opportunities for design innovation.

As shown in this diagram, preliminary calculations determined the volume of on-site material available for reuse and identified potential locations for use on-site in aggregate base courses for parking and lawn, and as the fill material for ramps. Avoiding hauling and disposal fees resulted in significant savings for the project.

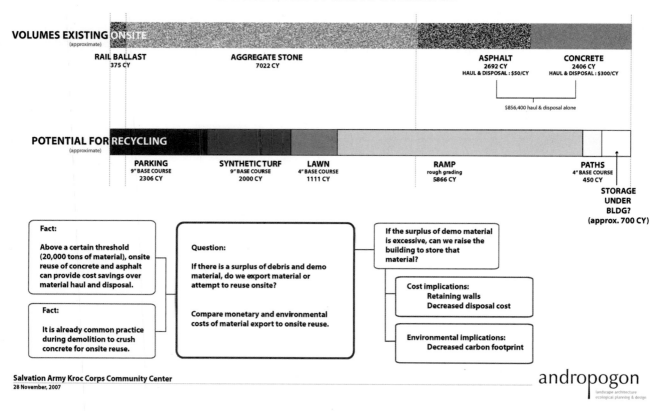

## MATERIAL RECYCLING STRATEGY

**VOLUMES EXISTING ONSITE**
(approximate)

RAIL BALLAST
375 CY

AGGREGATE STONE
7022 CY

ASPHALT
2692 CY
HAUL & DISPOSAL : $50/CY

CONCRETE
2406 CY
HAUL & DISPOSAL : $300/CY

$856,400 haul & disposal alone

**POTENTIAL FOR RECYCLING**
(approximate)

PARKING
9" BASE COURSE
2306 CY

SYNTHETIC TURF
9" BASE COURSE
2000 CY

LAWN
4" BASE COURSE
1111 CY

RAMP
rough grading
5866 CY

PATHS
4" BASE COURSE
450 CY

STORAGE
UNDER
BLDG?
(approx. 700 CY)

**Fact:**

Above a certain threshold (20,000 tons of material), onsite reuse of concrete and asphalt can provide cost savings over material haul and disposal.

**Fact:**

It is already common practice during demolition to crush concrete for onsite reuse.

**Question:**

If there is a surplus of debris and demo material, do we export material or attempt to reuse onsite?

Compare monetary and environmental costs of material export to onsite reuse.

If the surplus of demo material is excessive, can we raise the building to store that material?

**Cost implications:**
Retaining walls
Decreased disposal cost

**Environmental implications:**
Decreased carbon footprint

andropogon
landscape architecture
ecological planning & design

**Reclamation of a textile factory and mill town into a sustainable mixed-use urban neighborhood offering housing, office space, cultural facilities, canals, and a water garden**

---

**LILLE, FRANCE**

**DESIGNED BY**
Atelier de Paysages Bruel-Delmar
(Paris, France)

**DESIGNED AND IMPLEMENTED 2008 TO 2015**

**62 ACRES / 25 HECTARES**
Phase 1, consisting of office building, plaza, lawn, water garden: 6.9 acres / 2.8 hectares

# HAUTE DEÛLE RIVER BANKS

Along a former industrial canal of the Upper Deûle River in Lille, the site of a cotton mill is being transformed into a walkable neighborhood. The innovative development weaves together the histories of the site, the needs of the present, and the hopes of the future, using ecology and industry as the warp and weft of the urban design. Canals and a water garden draw on the industrial forms and materials of the site in a beautifully choreographed recovery of the ecological function of historic marshes.

Canals link water to garden, and the district to its history. They also provide opportunities for unplanned recreation.

Precast concrete pavers and a brick-and-basalt grid recall the scale and materials of the textile mills.

---

The Haute Deûle River Banks district uses water to guide residents and visitors through the neighborhood and to highlight pedestrian connections within the area and to the larger community. North-south canals draw visitors through the site to the Deûle Canal, and a central axis connects, via a new bridge, across the Deûle Canal to the island neighborhood of Bois-Blanc. Running east to west, a new dockside promenade activates the Deûle Canal and connects the district to the pedestrian infrastructure of Lille. At the heart of the district, historic mill buildings, a great lawn, and a water garden form an extraordinary urban core that affirms a commitment to global commerce while firmly rooting the development in its local context. The lawn and water garden draw on French garden traditions to reveal the textile industries of Lille while also recovering the function of the local marshes: improving water quality and providing flood storage.

Lille was settled along the Deûle River in a location where ecological systems met cultural needs. The river provided a swift and steady transportation system and water supply, while the surrounding marshes provided defensible ground to slow enemy attacks. The Deûle River flows north to join the Lys, which forms a portion of the border between France and Belgium, and ultimately connects to the North Sea at Antwerp. The Upper Deûle runs through chalk soils to the south, where historically it meandered and spread into wide marshes. The Lower Deûle flows through clay soils where the river became incised and clearly defined. Lille was situated near the end of the navigable river, connecting productive lands and global commerce.

This schematic diagram highlights the water infrastructure of the site. Water is piped (dashed lines) to canals (solid lines). In Phase 1, at the center of the diagram, all canals flow south to the water garden, which cleans the water before releasing it to the river (red arrow).

POSTINDUSTRIAL LANDSCAPES

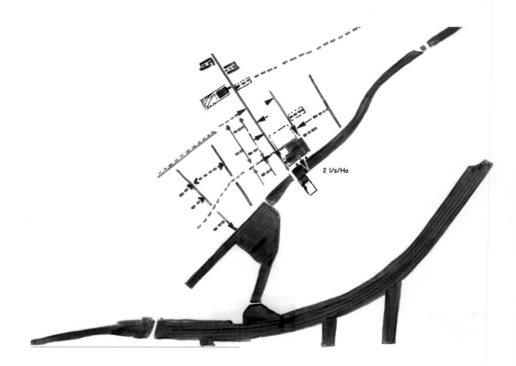

2 l/s/Ha

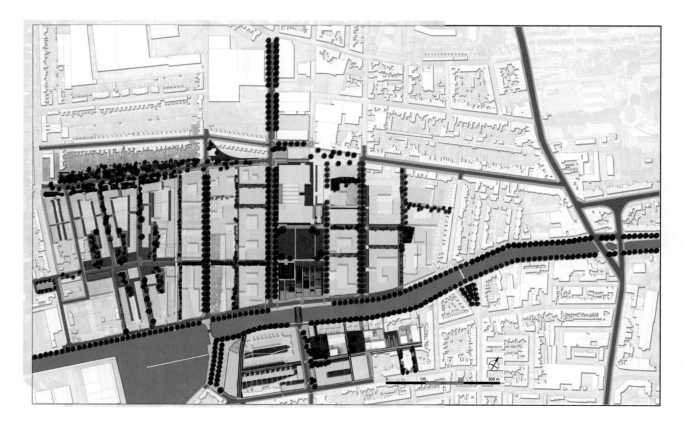

From the Middle Ages, Lille was known for its textiles and cloth trade. Early manufacturers spun and wove wool, and later cotton and flax. By the beginning of the twentieth century, the marshes south of town had mostly been drained, through a series of drying canals, to create land for expansive spinning and weaving mills. The land was patterned in long, thin lots divided by drainage canals perpendicular to the Deûle Canal. The Le Blan cotton mills, opened in 1872, covered more than 6 acres (2.4 hectares) and were surrounded by streets filled with workers' housing. Five-story brick buildings with tall Renaissance-style towers formed the central core of the complex, while long, low, parallel, skylit buildings adjacent to the canal contained the spinning and twisting machines. The mill closed in 1989, like many of the mills in Lille a casualty of the French textile crisis of the 1980s, when high taxes and rigid labor laws made French textile companies unable to compete in the global market.

The factory site and its adjoining worker housing district are undergoing reconstruction as a mixed-use district, with residential, retail, and office space. The aim is both urban and economic renewal. At its core is the first-phase project, with large public open spaces, streetscape and local canal improvements, and the renovated mill building. Throughout the site, the redevelopment of the Le Blan

The old textile mill (now the EuraTechnologies building), the great lawn, and the water garden, seen at the center of the district plan, are the heart of a new development organized around the Deûle Canal to the south and smaller canals that primarily run parallel to the tree-lined streets.

**95**

HAUTE DEÛLE RIVER BANKS

factory recovers two histories: the industrial history of the mills and the ecological history of the marshes.

The landscape reveals its industrial history through objects, layout, and materials. The historic buildings are the primary link to the textile manufacture. The brick buildings, with their elegant detailing and crenellated towers, have been connected with a glassed atrium and repurposed as offices. The nineteenth-century mill, with its iconic profile, provides the orienting center of the district; it faces an intersection where the two primary axes of the site converge on a paved events plaza. South of the mill buildings were once spinning and twisting mills—twenty long, narrow, connected buildings perpendicular to the canal. A portion of the spinning mill site is now a water garden, where six linear pools crossed with bridges recreate the footprint of the mills. And throughout the site, materials recall the industrial past. Canals are formed by black-limestone-filled gabions, finished with a Corten cap and crossed by steel bridges. Site furnishings throughout—benches, lights, bollards, bike racks—are made of rust-colored steel recalling the heavy machinery that once occupied the site. And on the ground, prefab concrete slabs edged with brick and cast basalt pavers reflect the materials and scale of the industrial buildings.

The recovery of the ecological history is even more extraordinary. As the draining of the marshes proved, water could be efficiently removed from the site. But now

The former textile mill is home to an innovative information technology incubator called EuraTechnologies.

———

Precast concrete paths span the garden, while steel landings give places to pause.

Benches, plazas, and steel landings provide areas for individual reflection or large gatherings.

water is celebrated as part of the identity of Lille and is used for orientation on the site and as wayfinding throughout. Local canals now draw pedestrians along the main axes of the site, toward the Deûle Canal and the central water garden. The canals and water garden are not merely visual elements; they provide the ecological function of marshes, an ecotype that has mostly been lost along the Upper Deûle. The braided wetlands—part river, part land—would have provided a range of ecological benefits: flood storage in heavy storms; pollution removal and water purification through filtration by plants and through sedimentation as water slowly moved through the marshes; water temperature regulation; and biodiversity, especially of plants and animals low on the food chain. Without wetlands, rivers are warmer and more polluted, and less hospitable for fish, small mammals, and birds. The Haute Deûle River Banks district recovers the function of the marshes in the forms of the industrial past. Canals align with roads, factories, and former drainage channels. They collect storm water from roads and buildings, and flow into the nearly 2-acre (0.8-hectare) water garden. Like a wetland, the water garden collects and treats the storm water before releasing it into the Deûle.

The district is organized as a series of valleys, canals, and ponds. Plazas and streets slope toward canals that run north-south. The canals provide a first stage in cleaning the rainwater as sediment settles out. They also provide nearly 20 inches (50 centimeters) of floodwater storage, a critical consideration for designers in the face of uncertain climate-change models, most of which predict higher-intensity storms in the coming decades. And they provide beautiful, plane-tree-lined routes through the district, an affirmation of the importance of water, of the industrial past (reflected in the stone and steel materials), and of a pleasant, walkable neighborhood. Everywhere, water is celebrated, from the structure of the district to elegantly detailed outflows of stepped white limestone.

The heart of the district is the north-south connection between the Deûle Canal and the historic mill buildings. Here, large public open spaces provide room for events, recreation, and socializing. There is a plaza adjacent to the buildings, and to the south, a great lawn unfolds to the water garden adjacent to the Deûle

This section shows the gentle slope of the water garden, which creates varying water depth and allows diverse plant communities to grow.

Canal. The garden itself is impressed into the land, gently sloping from a wet meadow adjacent to the great lawn to a depth of nearly 3 feet (1 meter) at the southern end. Concrete plank bridges cross the length of the water garden, dividing it into six separate pools. Thin steel bridges connect between the pools, leading to steel landings within the garden where visitors can pause, immersed in the sounds, smells, and colors of the marsh. The water garden, although designed for flood storage and to clean pollutants from the water, is meant to be, above all, a garden. Plantings are organized by phytoremediation qualities; depth of water; and color, with white, blue, yellow, and pink flowers of lilies, water hyacinth, and other wetland species. The concrete bridges orient visitors to the factory buildings and to the Deûle and the Bois-Blanc neighborhood beyond. And on the steel landings, educational signage informs visitors of the industrial past and the ecological future of the landscape.

The Haute Deûle River Banks district weaves industrial and ecological histories together with a vision of the future based in walkable neighborhoods, clean technology employment, and cities that provide ecological function and climate-change readiness with beauty and grace. The design is strongly rooted in place: in the marshes of the Deûle, in the textile industry of Lille, and in the traditions of French garden design. Water parterres, strong geometry, industrial materials, bold colors, and long visual axes connect the district firmly to its place and history while creating a forward-looking neighborhood.

Aquatic and marginal species were selected primarily for their ability to filter out pollutants from the water.

**Self-financed community park with earth art, playgrounds, recreation paths and fields, fishing ponds, wetland, and a model boating lake**

---

**NORTHOLT, WEST LONDON, ENGLAND**

**DESIGNED BY**
Peter Fink, artist, and Igor Marko, architect, FoRM Associates (London)

Peter Neal, ecologist

LDA Design (London), landscape architect

**COMPLETED IN 2008**

**45.7 ACRES / 18.5 HECTARES**

# NORTHALA FIELDS PARK

At Northala Fields Park, serious site and social constraints have been inverted into a new form of park. The site was noisy, windy, polluted from the adjacent highway, and prone to flooding, and the borough lacked funding for construction. The designers proposed bringing in hundreds of thousands of tons of clean fill to create innovative topographic sculpture, charging tipping fees to generate revenue. The resulting iconic hills and serpentine waterway solve the pragmatic problems of the park while also providing recreation opportunities, biodiversity, and extraordinary earth forms that attract and energize people.

Nearly 2 million cubic yards (1.5 million cubic meters) of construction debris structure the earth mounds at Northala Fields Park.

---

Wetlands filter water
before it joins a local
stream.

———

Water flows through
six increasingly irregular
fish ponds, then to a
wetland that provides
flood storage.

Northala Fields Park, at
the center of the district
plan, connects to a
regional system of parks
and is part of a master
plan to provide more
active recreation areas.

An early sketch shows
the main landscape types:
woodland, grassland,
and wetland.

The hills buffer the
fields and ponds from
the noise and pollution
of the highway.

West of London, adjacent to the A40 highway, four earth mounds rise enigmatically toward the sky. Motorists would be forgiven if, as they drove by, they thought these were ancient landforms. Wildflower meadows bloom on some of the slopes, and a path spirals up the tallest to an observation platform where people look out over the surrounding landscape. What appear to be ancient structures on the land, sacred mounds or burial sites, are something at once far more pragmatic and elegantly poetic. They are spoil heaps—piles of rubble from construction and demolition projects—and their construction funded the park around them while also creating a major piece of land art that functions as a landmark for West London.

Northala Fields Park is the result of a design competition in 2000. The Borough of Ealing, in west London, purchased the site in 1997 but didn't have the funding to develop a park. Seeking innovative, low-cost ideas, the competition brief asked for a land art approach. FoRM Associates, recognizing that the site was prone to flooding, realized that land art would not be possible with a balanced cut-and-fill approach; additional imported fill would be needed to create the visual icon, environmental buffer, and dry fields the site required. If material needed to be imported, why not generate revenue from that and maximize the potential for both income and landform creation? The result was an innovative strategy of generation that recognized the opportunities inherent in the material processes of construction. Rather than a landfill being the end of the line after construction, the designers proposed landfill as construction, resulting in the generation of revenue, topographic material, and local identity.

The imported material was sculpted into four circular hills ranging from 60 to 100 feet (20 to 30 meters) high, which buffer the park from the highway's noise,

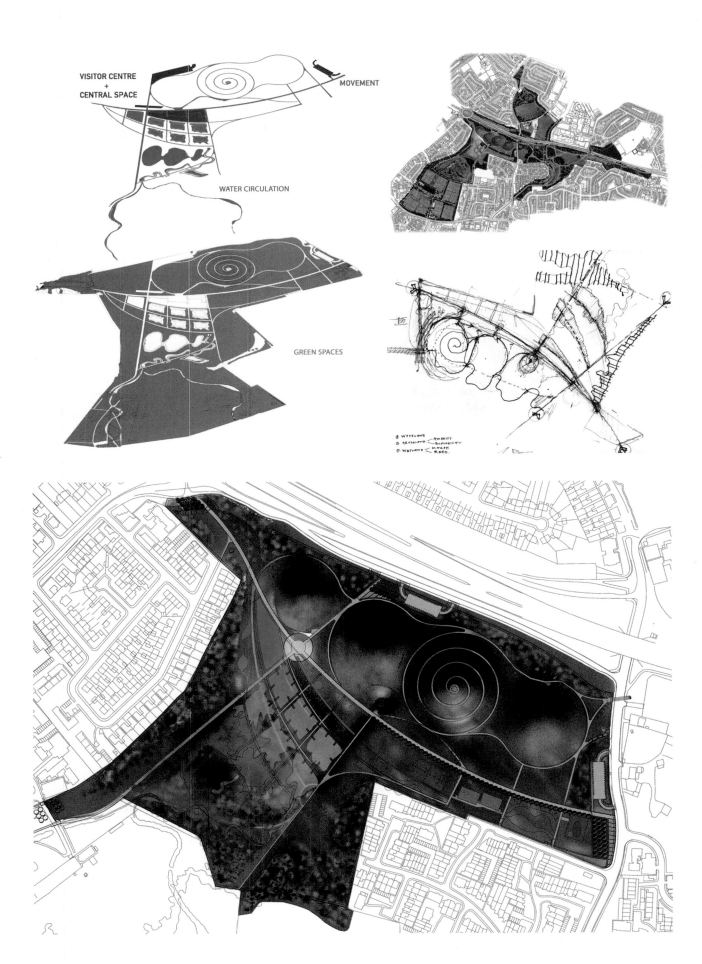

VISITOR CENTRE
+
CENTRAL SPACE

MOVEMENT

WATER CIRCULATION

GREEN SPACES

pollution, and visual impact. The topography creates new opportunities for recreation. The hills are popular for walking, running, biking, and sledding, and they provide a new vantage point to the London skyline. The newly sculpted watercourse provides stocked fishing ponds and a model boating pond, and two new playgrounds have proved very popular. The topography creates ecological opportunities as well, with a variety of meadows, woodlands, and scrub created in the previously flat and flood-prone site. Rainwater is now directed away from fields, into new wetlands that slow and clean the water before it joins a local stream.

The park's innovative strategy of self-funded construction emerges from the recognition that landscape construction is embedded in a web of material use and generation. Rather than viewing the site as closed, where cut and fill must be balanced, or as a starting point for a process that ends with waste bound for a landfill, the designers understood Northala Fields Park as part of a network of urban construction where some sites generate material that may be useful at others. The borough accepted clean fill from demolition and construction projects around London, including the demolition of the old Wembley Stadium and a local mall, and rubble from Heathrow's Terminal 5 construction. In addition to providing the material for the earth art hills, the fill also generated the necessary funding for the park construction. The tipping fees from nearly 2 million cubic yards (1.5 million cubic meters) of rubble funded the project cost of nearly $10 million (£5.5 million). In the process, the park construction also had a significant positive environmental impact, saving an estimated 160,000 truck trips of more than 200 miles (320 kilometers) to outlying fill sites.

The park uses a variety of recycled material, demonstrating the range of scales of recycling possible, from low-impact on-site reuse to industrial reuse with higher embedded energy. On-site material reclamation is a frequently employed form of recycling, which obviously can only be undertaken at sites with useful preexisting material; at Northala Fields, granite cobble paving was repurposed for paths. Site-to-site material reuse allows a similar repurposing, but sources need to be identified in the region. Demolished concrete was repurposed into crushed concrete paths, and larger chunks were used to fill gabions for retaining walls on the spiral path and gabion benches throughout the park. Reclaimed railway ties were milled into timber for site furnishings, including benches and trash cans. A third form of material recycling involves industrial reconstruction of materials such as plastic or glass into new products. At Northala Fields, recycled plastic was used for the fishing platforms and path edging, providing durable, stable material in wet environments.

FoRM Associates wanted to integrate the new park into its ecological context and also provide new opportunities for biodiversity and habitat patches. The park is organized conceptually into concentric rings of habitat types: water, marginal aquatics, meadow, marginal shrub, and woods. Existing remnant woodlands were incorporated into larger woods around the edges of the park, acting as filters between the open meadows and the surrounding roads and neighborhoods. Meadows are the dominant habitat at the park, with a range of different plant communities—resulting from different soils, plantings, and maintenance regimes—highlighting the different meadow forms native to the region. The park is close to

The hills are popular for sledding in the winter.

NORTHALA FIELDS PARK

the Royal Air Force Northolt airfield, so the habitat patches were designed primarily for smaller songbirds, to avoid attracting larger birds that could be harmed by, or pose a risk to, airplanes. Initial designs called for three large lakes for boating, fishing, and habitat; these were divided into several smaller ponds and wetlands to discourage large birds from landing and taking off. Storm water and groundwater flow through six fishing ponds, a model boating pond, and several habitat ponds before entering a marsh and stream that rejoins the local water system.

While integrating into natural systems and processes, the park is primarily a significant urban and cultural resource. It is a carefully balanced urban habitat that includes passive and active recreation, habitat patches that provide human access to natural processes and education, and patches that are less accessible to humans. The park paths connect to adjacent parks and recreation routes within the Northolt and Greenford Countryside Park, a 250-acre (100-hectare) open space network. While only the tallest hill has a path to the top, visitors seem compelled to climb each hill, and climbers have created an informal path linking the four peaks. Two playgrounds provide choices for children. In one, colorful, small-scale mounds echo the larger earthworks, play structures provide activities for children, and timber-framed planting beds provide seating for adults as well as informal balance beams for children. In the other, nature play is encouraged, with timber structures in the form of dragonflies and seashells, and boulders, timber,

Meadows are the dominant habitat, with different species mixes resulting from different soils, seed mixes, and mowing regimes.

**106**

and concrete-filled gabion blocks creating opportunities for unstructured play. (The gabion seats and retaining walls seem especially popular with children for climbing, balancing, and enthusiastic jumping.) Seating areas in the meadows and semiformal planting beds are opportunities for passive recreation, as is the observation platform at the top of the tallest hill. There, people come to talk, eat lunch, or just watch the landscape, and the hill has been used for sunrise prayer groups on holy days.

Like the gabion walls from which children launch themselves with joy and delight, the realities of construction waste reuse and project finance have been used at Northala Fields Park as a springboard to poetic earthworks, ecology, and play.

Colorful mounds in the playground echo the landforms beyond.

NORTHALA FIELDS PARK

# VEGETATED ARCHITECTURE

## Living Roofs and Walls

Park TMB in
Barcelona, Spain.

**THERE IS A SPECIAL DELIGHT** in a green roof, a secret garden in the sky. To climb a staircase, open a door to a roof, and step out into a lush *giardino segreto*; to be surrounded by ferns and flowers, 30 feet above the ground; to watch birds and bats swoop precipitously close to a parapet is a unique urban joy. As green roofs and living walls become more common, we have seen an increasing sophistication and beauty in them. They are becoming designed sites rather than simply pragmatic solutions to technical problems.

The earliest green roofs were on the turf houses of Scandinavia. Wood-framed houses were clad in thick stone and turf walls, the turf blocks laid in intricate patterns like bricks. The roofs were constructed of planks over rafters, covered by thin layers of bark, and finished with two layers of sod, the first grass-down, and the second grass-up. The mass of the soil and the slope of the roof kept most water out of the home, but sod houses were, by all descriptions, rather damp in spite of their picturesque appearance.

It wasn't until the 1970s in Germany that a modern green roof system was developed, and they remain largely unchanged today. A waterproof membrane, a drainage layer, a soil layer, and plants make up most green roofs, whether thin or thick, flat or sloped, custom or modular. The first modern green roofs were installed primarily for environmental benefits and typically had a thin layer of soil and drought-tolerant plants such as sedums and sempervivums. In many settings, this is all that is needed to reap a host of economic and environmental benefits. These extensive plantings are well suited for roofs that are not accessed often, where the primary goal is not social or aesthetic (and in fact, for roofs that are seen but not accessed, the wide variety of drought-tolerant plants available gives spectacular aesthetic results). For more ambitious living roofs, deeper soils and irrigation are used to extend the planting palette, including shrubs and trees, and planting is mixed with paving to provide activity areas. The conflicting desires for deep soils, often around trees, and thin soils, for less weight on the roof, can lead to creative roof designs, with steps, hills, and terraces used to increase soil volume, resulting in complex, multilayered planting designs.

Similarly, the first green walls were simply buildings with ivy or another vine growing up them. Vegetated walls are generally divided into two categories: green facades and living walls. Green facades are composed of vines or other climbing plants, often rooted in the ground but sometimes in planters, or cascading over a parapet. Living walls are a continuous vegetated surface—panels, mats, and grids are common construction techniques.

The host of benefits that vegetated architecture—living roofs and walls—can provide is well documented. A building owner might want to clad the roof or walls with plants for a number of pragmatic and ethical reasons. And that is where design innovation steps in. Roof gardens and living walls are vegetated canvases, gardens to shelter and delight. Whether designed as a lawn or a meadow, a thin plane of color or a lush garden, the roofs and walls that follow take on the challenge of making memorable landscapes that charm and engage the visitor, and often give back to the local environment through habitat for birds, butterflies, insects, and microinvertebrates.

The European Environment Agency living wall was a temporary structure installed in the summer of 2010. It featured a modular steel frame that sat lightly on the face of a historic office building, filled with panels holding soil and plants. The structure, soil pockets, and integrated irrigation provide a model for a simple living wall retrofit. But it is the use of the technical in support of the ethical and aesthetic that inspires. The planting design, in the form of a biodiversity map of Europe, sought to both educate visitors about the significance of biodiversity and bring biodiversity into the heart of Copenhagen, using native flowers and fruits to entice birds and insects. The vertical map garden was a lush, colorful tapestry that enlivened the public square.

**Temporary green wall installation demonstrating the ability to increase vegetation and biodiversity within urban areas**

——

**COPENHAGEN, DENMARK**

**DESIGNED BY**
Johanna Rossbach, Mangor & Nagel Arkitektfirma (Copenhagen), architect

Ramboll Denmark (Copenhagen), engineers

Green Fortune (Stockholm), green wall

Life Sciences at the University of Copenhagen (LIFE)

the Municipality of Copenhagen

**ON DISPLAY MAY THROUGH OCTOBER 2010**

**2,500 SQUARE FEET / 230 SQUARE METERS**

# EUROPEAN ENVIRONMENT AGENCY

Immediately after planting, the greens of foliage predominated.

But within weeks, flowers were blooming, covering the façade in a tapestry of color.

——

For six months in the summer of 2010, one of the main squares in Copenhagen was transformed by a living façade into a locus of ecological education. The European Environment Agency (EEA) used its highly visible façade to increase awareness of biodiversity in Europe and of the need for vegetation in urban centers. More than five thousand annuals created a living map of the biodiversity zones of Europe, with silver and white foliage and flowers

representing the northern zones of lower biodiversity, and yellows and reds representing the biodiversity hotspots along the Mediterranean Sea.

The EEA offices are on the northeastern edge of Kongens Nytorv (King's New Square), the largest and one of the most prominent public squares in Copenhagen, and a busy site of outdoor exhibitions, high school graduation festivities, and winter ice skating. With its location in the urban center, the building is quite visible in the daily life of the city. As part of the UN's International Year of Biodiversity, the EEA decided to create a living façade on its building. The structure was the first of its kind in Denmark, intended to showcase the importance of natural ecosystems, biodiversity, and urban vegetation. The project was meant to be visibly artificial, to clearly demonstrate that urban constructions can provide ecosystem services and contribute to biodiversity. It was a demonstration project showing building owners that by adding vegetation to existing buildings, they could provide habitat, reduce noise, improve air quality, and increase urban quality of life.

The EEA façade provided a visually stunning example of living wall technology and highlighted some opportunities of the material. A five-story steel structure

The wall was installed on a demountable frame that rested lightly on the façade of the building.

**116**

provided a grid for the vegetated installation, whose bands of color drifted across the neoclassical building to create a biodiversity map of Europe. Because the project was temporary, the designers were able to select plants whose flowers and foliage created the greatest visual impact, without worrying about hardiness or longevity. And while planted walls offer environmental and acoustic benefits, it is their visual impact—their potential for education, place making, and urban excitement—that makes them extraordinary in cities. Additionally, the EEA system had

In the planting plan, each band of color represents a biodiversity zone, and each is planted with two to six species in the corresponding color range.

Det Europæiske Miljøagentur

The felt pockets were attached to a rebar frame in modular panels.

—

More than five thousand plants were used, with colors ranging from silvers and grays to represent the northern regions, to bright reds and pinks to stand for the biodiversity hotspots of the Mediterranean.

Once the structure was in place, plants were hand planted into felt pockets.

Native species were used, to accentuate the potential of green walls to increase habitat in cities.

an unusual planting design approach. Many designers of living walls treat them as unique urban microclimates, selecting plants based on similar ecosystems such as cliffs and rocky escarpments. The EEA façade instead sought to integrate the building into the surrounding ecological context. It used native plants, which few living walls employ, with an intention to increase habitat for birds and pollinators within the city.

The project faced several technical challenges, the two most significant of which were applying a living façade to an existing building in a noninvasive manner and irrigating the plants in Copenhagen's dry summer. The technical solutions achieved provide examples for more permanent structures in other locations.

The EEA offices are located in a five-story building with five structural bays on the courtyard façade. The first two floors have flush windows, while the third and fourth floor windows are recessed. At the third floor, that recess creates a narrow balcony, which provided the opportunity for the key connection between the existing building and the applied living wall system. The system was essentially a free-standing modular steel grid hung from the balcony and carefully stabilized without damaging the existing building. Six steel columns hung from the balcony, providing the primary load-bearing structure for the living wall. Rods and plates braced the columns at each floor, holding the living façade steady just inches away from the neoclassical details beneath. A series of thirty-five panels was mounted to the columns, providing the framework for the planted map as well as lateral

stability for the frame. Each panel contained a frame of steel tubes and angles and an infill mesh of steel rods, and was bolted to the steel columns.

Before being installed on the columns, the panels were fitted with scrims and felt pockets. Where the panels covered windows, printed scrims blended in with the surrounding foliage while allowing light into the building and filtered views out. Where the panels covered masonry, the planted map was installed. Plywood panels with felt pockets held the growing medium. To maintain the plants during the warm dry summer, water pipes were attached to the steel columns to distribute water through a drip irrigation system that was integrated into the felt pocket system. Plants grew in a mix of "leca-nuts" (a term for light expanded clay aggregate) and standard topsoil. Leca is formed by heating small pieces of clay until they expand, forming a material similar in composition to pumice that reduces the weight of the soil, provides air pockets, and retains some water.

More than five thousand plants, representing twenty species of annuals, were hand planted into the felt pockets. Plants were chosen based on several criteria. The primary need was representational, to mark the various biodiversity regions of Europe. Northern Europe, with up to five hundred species per 3,900 square miles (10,000 square kilometers), was represented in three bands of silvery foliage or white-flowering plants. Central Europe, with five hundred to fifteen hundred species per 3,900 square miles (10,000 square kilometers), was represented in two zones of plants with glossy green foliage and yellow and pink flowers. And the most biodiverse regions of southern Europe, with up to four thousand species per 3,900 square miles (10,000 square kilometers), were represented in three zones of lush green and red foliage, with red, blue, and purple flowers, and some fruiting plants such as strawberries. The plants grew, bloomed, and fruited over the summer installation period, creating a slowly shifting display of color and depth.

The living wall at the European Environment Agency was a temporary installation. As such, it did not need to address some of the more vexing problems of living walls, such as plant maintenance and mortality, and maintenance access to the plants and building. However, the designers did have to solve some difficulties, including irrigation and soil containment. The modular frame system, with felt pockets and integrated irrigation, provides a model for quick and cost-efficient installation. The project had an added challenge in that it was a retrofit on an existing building and could not leave a permanent mark on the building. For living walls on new buildings, or permanent installations, the structure is less complicated. In the end, this enchanting installation demonstrated the possibility of using living walls to increase vegetation and biodiversity within urban areas.

The European Environment Agency façade enlivened the Kongens Nytorv public square for six months.

**121**

**Sloped roof lawn at Lincoln Center's north plaza, offering public open space above a new building**

———

**NEW YORK, NEW YORK**

**DESIGNED BY**
Diller Scofidio + Renfro
(New York City)

**COMPLETED IN 2010**

**10,800 SQUARE FEET /
1,000 SQUARE METERS**

# HYPAR PAVILION

On a sunny summer day, people lounge, read, picnic, and social-ize on the gently sloping lawn at the northern edge of Lincoln Center. The lawn is also the roof of a restaurant. One corner of the roof slopes down to the plaza level where long, low stairs pro-vide access, while at the other end the lawn soars above the glass façade of the restaurant. The design adds the client's desired pro-gram space without sacrificing open space and provides a model for new green spaces in urban centers.

The plaza at Lincoln Center formerly covered the street; now access is clear and open, and the green lawn dips invitingly to the street.

———

**123**

The pavilion is conceived
as a segment sliced and
lifted from the plaza.

New York has a wide range of public open spaces, from icons like Central Park and Bryant Park to smaller pocket parks and an extensive network of privately owned public spaces. However, a constant tension exists between development and open space; the desire to maximize sellable or leasable space is tempered by a need for places for people to be outdoors in the city. As part of a major renovation of Lincoln Center, the designers were asked to include a new restaurant as well as public open space. By using the roof of the new restaurant as a lawn, Diller Scofidio + Renfro performed a magic trick: adding a building while maintaining the existing amount of open space. To do that, they laid out a rectangle of grass and peeled up two corners to create a volume beneath it. In the seemingly simple design, they also created some vexing technical challenges.

Lincoln Center is one of New York's iconic landscapes, but one that needed renovations and improvements as it aged. The art and performance complex was designed as a citadel for the arts, elevated above the urban chaos. But over time, that remove felt more like a disconnect. The center needed better access from the street; more clarity of traffic flow for deliveries, taxis, and pedestrians; and

The green carpet touches down at the southwest corner in a broad stair.

better circulation and sightlines between its three plazas. A team of designers and consultants was hired to improve the center and connect it more seamlessly with the city, and also to provide better visitor services through new program elements. One of those, a new restaurant, was to be located in the north plaza, adjacent to the center's movie theater.

The original north plaza, designed by Dan Kiley, connected across West 65th Street to the Julliard School and Alice Tully Hall. The 200-foot-wide bridge, while elegant, made West 65th Street dark and unpleasant, and cut the plaza off from the city. In a major alteration of Kiley's design, the plaza-bridge was removed and replaced with a narrow pedestrian bridge, the sidewalks were widened on 65th Street, and new stairs to the east and west were added to connect the street below to the plaza above. Alice Tully Hall used to be the north edge of the plaza;

now Hypar Pavilion creates that edge. The building also helps to buffer the plaza from the increased street noise, and the roof lawn creates a parklike space where a raised planter of plane trees once stood. As the roof lawn cantilevers out over 65th Street, it creates a canopy over the sidewalk that defines the street and invites pedestrians up to explore.

Hypar Pavilion is an enchanting floating carpet of lawn hovering over a glass box. It solves many problems of the Kiley design and is a contemporary voice in dialogue with the midcentury work. The gentle slope of the lawn allows easy pedestrian access to the roof by way of amphitheater-like long, low steps. The undulating forms create comfortable areas for socializing and relaxing, even in a very urban context. The roof lawn is a hyperbolic parabaloid, or hypar—a saddle-shaped surface with two opposite corners raised and the alternate two lowered. This creates a gently curving roof with the feel of rolling hills, a pastoral moment in the concrete jungle. It also results in continuously changing slopes on the roof, from level at the seat of the saddle to 1:12 at the access point and 3:12 at the steepest areas. This creates an elegant form and a welcome variety of lawn options, from nearly flat for a picnic to steeper slopes suitable for reclining.

But the roof lawn also creates technical challenges of soil stability, compaction, and safety. First there is the challenge of keeping soils from slipping down the steeper slopes. On vegetated roofs with simpler geometry, linear baffles can be used perpendicular to the slope, or cellular structures across the entire roof, to hold the soil in place. But with the varied slope of the roof, a stiff material would not work.

In the new design, the same general elements hold the same general composition as in the original design: trees to the south, reflecting pool in the center, and a northern boundary, now formed by Hypar Pavilion.

———

As this model of the form shows, the hypar (hyperbolic paraboloid) surface turns the lawn from a plane into rolling hills, a flying carpet.

Another challenge was the anticipated heavy pedestrian traffic at this popular site. With heavy use, soils could compact and slip, effectively creating landslides and wearing steplike depressions into steeper slopes. Both challenges—soil movement and heavy traffic—called for a structured, cellular system holding the soil rather than baffles. The manufacturer, Hydrotech, worked with the designers to develop a new product that could accommodate the variable slope of the roof. The product is effectively a deep net of perforated plastic strips. The material can flex to cover variable curves, while the perforations allow root growth and water flow between cells. The net is fastened to the roof, anchoring the lawn into place.

While the roof dips down to plaza level for access, at its highest points it is 11 feet above the plaza and 23 feet above the street. The designers needed to include railings on all sides that wouldn't interrupt the appearance of the clean sweep of grass. On the east and west sides of the pavilion, the roof ends flush to the building, and the glass façade of the pavilion slips up above the roof to create a glass railing. On the north and south sides, deep cantilevers prevent this use of the façade glass as railing. The designers chose to use a stainless steel stanchion and mesh system that visually evaporates against the sky. Here, too, the complex slopes created difficulty. The line of the rail is clean, and the angle between mesh and stanchion is constant. But the angle of the stanchion to the lawn shifts continuously, so there is no standard detail for that connection; the designers had to develop a series of unique stanchion profiles and connection details.

Hypar Pavilion is a welcome improvement to the north edge of the plaza, solving real problems of access and visibility in a successful edit of Kiley's original design. But changes to the southern portion of the plaza renewed a professional debate about the destruction of historic works of landscape architecture. Revision of a grove of trees there to echo the slope of the roof lawn eliminated key elements of Kiley's design without significantly improving the plaza. The original design was a field of square travertine planters, partially sunken to create low seating around quartets of plane trees. These have been replaced with a single, sloped, gravel-floored grove of plane trees with a folded concrete border that continuously warps from the proportions of a bench to a chaise longue. The current design is relaxed and casual, with moveable seating reminiscent of Bryant Park. But Kiley's design—a clean, modern field with an elegant formality—was a masterpiece of modernist landscape architecture, and many lament its loss.

Regardless, the lawn roof of Hypar Pavilion shows the potential of urban roofs to double as accessible open space. Through the innovation of a sloped roof that touches down at ground level, the designers have seemingly doubled the area of the pavilion, sliding building program under an undulating lawn. The pavilion provides a continuous urban landscape that connects street, plaza, and sky.

The lawn roof provides a pastoral foreground to views of Lincoln Center.

The slope of the new grove echoes the slope of the lawn. While the grove is pleasant, the loss of the Kiley design has been lamented by some critics.

129

HYPAR PAVILION

**Urban park with spaces for
play and active recreation built
on the roof of a bus depot**

—

**BARCELONA, SPAIN**

**DESIGNED BY**
Jaime Coll, Coll-Leclerc (Barcelona),
architects

Teresa Galí-Izard, Arquitectura
Agronomia (Barcelona), landscape
architects

Manel Comas, engineer

Xavier Badia, technical architect

David Garcia, BIS Arquitectes,
structural consultant

**COMPLETED IN 2006**

**4.94 ACRES / 2 HECTARES**

# PARK TMB

This park atop a bus depot in the Barcelona neighborhood of
Horta is a vibrant example of a living roof performing not only
a technical function (managing storm water and insulating the
building) but also a social function. As a park, it stands out as a
colorful and dynamic space for play and passive recreation. As
a living roof, it is extraordinary in that the design synthesizes the
park and roof qualities of the project, with neither aspect domi-
nating the other. The park mediates between the city and a natural reserve to the north, turning a potential eyesore into a vibrant
urban amenity.

The roof of a bus
depot has become a
vibrant threshold to a
natural reserve.

—

The Horta neighborhood north of central Barcelona was connected to downtown by the Ronda de Dalt ring road built for the 1992 Olympic games. The neighborhood sits at the foot of the Collserola mountain range, home to a 20,000-acre (8,000-hectare) natural reserve park. Construction of the ring road required massive earthworks, leaving leveled areas adjacent to the new road in some districts. In the Horta neighborhood, the foot of the Collserola mountain range had been terraced for a staging area for the construction.

In 2000, the Transports Metropolitans de Barcelona (TMB) decided to locate a bus depot for three hundred buses at the location, taking advantage of the large expanse of leveled ground and easy access to the ring road. The building contains 646,000 square feet (60,000 square meters) of parking on three semi-underground levels tucked into the hillside. The building has a 215,000-square-foot (20,000-square-meter) roof, and the decision was made to return that expanse to public use through the creation of a park. The park provides much-needed public amenities and also creates an entry point to the Collserola Natural Park that is easily accessed via public transportation. The rectangular park is organized into circular program zones of a variety of materials—sand, concrete, grass, rubber—separated by sinuous bike and pedestrian paths. The interstitial spaces are planted in the materials of the surrounding Collserola mountain range: grass, pine, and bamboo.

Park TMB gracefully resolves two main constraints: drainage and weight. These constraints are common to vegetated roofs but exacerbated in this building, with its expansive size and the need for long spans of open space in the building beneath. The designers grappled with the technical issues of moving storm water and minimizing roof loads. These constraints led to creative organizational strategies for this urban park and to opportunities for both technical and formal innovation in the resulting dimpled landscape.

Heavy fall rainstorms in Barcelona can create flash urban inundations. The rapid removal of water from these heavy storms is important in any urban park but especially here, where the weight of water is a significant load on the building roof. The rectangular building was designed with a gentle roof slope to the south and a more noticeable slope to the east and west. Gutters are positioned to the east and west, so all storm water had to move in those directions across the length of the building. Using city storm water standards, drain inlets needed to be provided for every 2,150 to 4,300 square feet (200 to 400 square meters), and the pipes had to be a minimum 16 inches (400 millimeters) in diameter.

The need to remove water led the designers to conceive of the roof as a series of funnels to quickly gather and remove heavy rains, situated on a ground of

The park is an extension of the Collserola mountain range and brings the native vegetation into the city.

Details throughout the park anticipate active use; the railing design accommodates a range of postures and purposes.

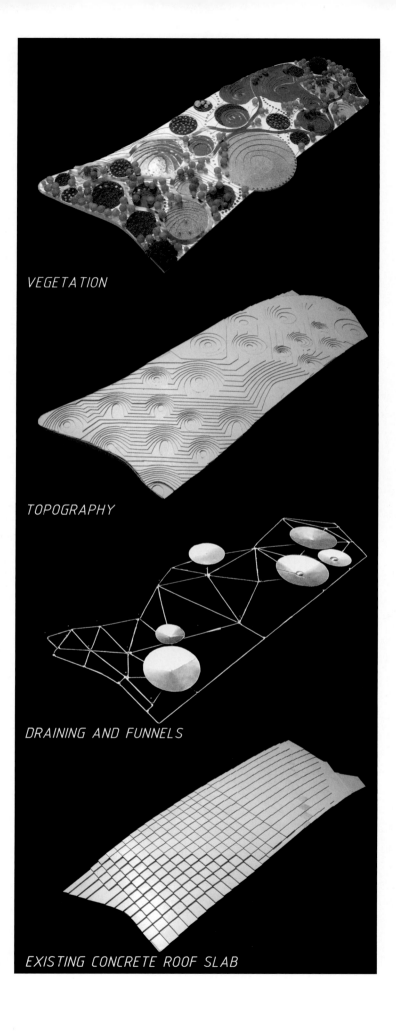

VEGETATION

TOPOGRAPHY

DRAINING AND FUNNELS

EXISTING CONCRETE ROOF SLAB

The exploded axono-
metric shows how the
dimples mediate the roof
structure and organize
the program and planting.
The concrete roof slopes
to the east and west; the
funnels quickly collect
and remove rainwater,
while the interstitial areas
are a rolling topography
of grass and pine.

interstitial space where storm water could percolate and disperse more slowly. Twenty-six concave basins of varying sizes serve a variety of functions in the daily life of the park and act as large storm-water collection areas in rainstorms. The basins have two types of surface materials—hardscapes and vegetation, referred to by the architects as cold and warm landscapes, which provide space for a wide range of active and passive recreation, from biking and skateboarding to picnicking and sunbathing.

Between the funnels, the interstitial space is wrinkled and dimpled to gently collect storm water, allowing it to pool and percolate. These areas are planted with two types of vegetation—hyparrhenia (grass) and a pine-and-grass mix. Both are indigenous to the surrounding Collserola mountain range and extend the vegetation of the hills into the city.

The two water collection systems operate at two different depths. The funnels collect water surficially and conduct it through drains and pipes to scuppers. The

Clearly visible in this photograph during planting, twenty-six circles imagine a wide range of programs on sand, gravel, concrete, ivy, lawn, and bougainvillea.

**135**

PARK TMB

wrinkled landscapes allow water to filter through the soil, after which it is conducted horizontally along the surface of the waterproof membrane below. The funnel landscape was intended to gather water into two basins from which it would be distributed for irrigation. However, for a variety of reasons, not the least of which was the weight of the water, this reuse program was abandoned.

To generate the concave slopes needed for water collection, accommodate the large drainage pipes, support extensive park plantings, and divide the park into smaller landscape rooms, a fairly thick base was required, some of which needed to be soil for the plants. Reconciling this park need with the underlying building led to the second, technical innovation: a thin concrete vault topography.

The bus depot below has a very large structural bay of 46 square feet (14 square meters), with very long spans supporting the roof. The roof itself, without the soil and plants, is 39-inch-thick (1-meter-thick) concrete, so the park design had to be as lightweight as possible. Additionally, the park requires maintenance access for trucks, adding significantly to the live loads and further reducing the weight allowed for the park. The roof is divided into 23-foot-by-23-foot (7-meter-by-7-meter) slabs that step down a gentle slope to the south and more strongly to the east and west, creating a blocky underlying topography. The design had to create depth without weight while smoothing out the pixelated topography of the roof.

After several technical solutions were proposed and rejected, the designers and engineers decided to use plastic formwork caissons of varying heights that could

The funnels are constructed over concrete rings, while the interstitial space sits on thin concrete over lightweight plastic caissons.

———

The different areas have varied ground surfaces, anticipating a wide variety of uses. The colorful rubber surfacing can be used for dance or gymnastics.

**137**

PARK TMB

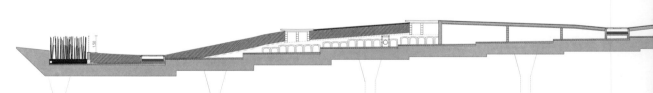

be stacked up to 55 inches (140 centimeters) high. With 39 inches (1 meter) of lightweight soil, this allowed topographic definition of up to 95 inches (240 centimeters). The caissons, 20 inches (50 centimeters) square, give a more fine-grained resolution to the topography of the roof. They are covered with a thin stabilizing layer of concrete, effectively creating a hollow vaulted structure between roof deck and park surface. The soil is placed above the concrete and smooths out the contours of the park.

All vegetated roofs need to contend with drainage and weight. The climate of Barcelona and the reality of a bus depot foregrounded those challenges at the Horta bus depot park. The layered solutions of pixelated topography, slow sub-surficial drainage, and rapid surficial removal use the challenges of vegetated architecture as a springboard for formal and technical innovations. In addition, the park resolves several dualities of the site. The two forms of water collection reflect the two contexts: the funnels are informed by the artificial and technical nature of the roof, while the wrinkled landscapes in between reflect the natural park to the north.

Grass funnels provide areas for passive recreation and picnics.

———

The section shows how the roof is divided into blocky, stepped platforms. Lightweight caissons create a micro-topography that smooths the surface and directs water to the funnels.

**139**

PARK TMB

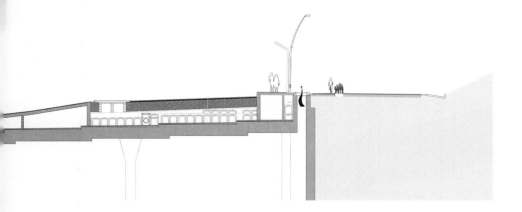

**Five rooftop terraces in an office complex, each an urban canvas with its own striking look and purpose**

———

**DEN BOSCH,
THE NETHERLANDS**

**DESIGNED BY**
Buro Sant en Co (The Hague),
landscape architects

De Architecten Cie
(Amsterdam), architects

**COMPLETED IN 2008**

**129,000 SQUARE FEET /
12,000 SQUARE METERS**

# ESSENT ROOFGARDENS

At the headquarters of Essent, the largest energy company in the Netherlands, five green roofs help provide access to and orientation within a substantially expanded building. Buro Sant en Co designed these green roofs to take advantage of their visual quality. Office workers have an aerial view of the terraces, which are designed as graphic parterres, each with a distinct character and function. The terraces are urban canvases, providing sites of representation, orientation, and identity.

The Essent living roofs use the unusual microclimates and weight constraints of green roofs as design inspiration. Here, wood steps raise the ground level to provide rooting space for trees.

———

141

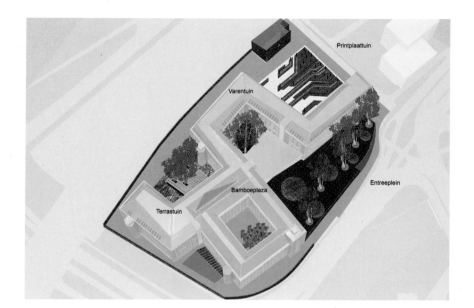

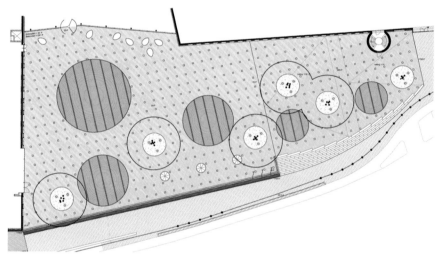

The blocky S of the new building and the courtyard of the old building are clear in the axonometric. The former courtyard, once a car park, now encloses a bamboo-filled atrium. A sunken parking garage was added to the west and north, capped with the new office wing. The folds of the new building frame four green roofs, each with a unique identity.

The entry plaza plan shows the area scattered with plantings like raindrops.

The patio garden was planned as a sunny open space where employees can eat or relax.

**142**

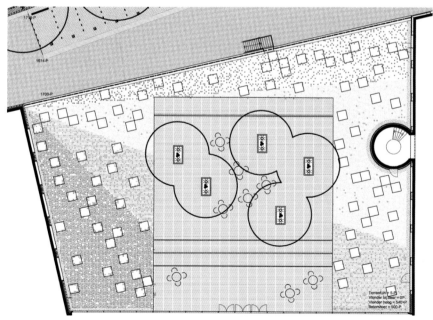

In a major expansion of their headquarters, Essent added 260,000 square feet (24,000 square meters) of office space to their existing 130,000-square-foot (12,000-square-meter) building. The original building, a square castlelike form with a central courtyard, faces onto the Dommel River to the east. The expansion added a new wing to the west, with two stories of underground parking forming a rectangular plinth beneath a folded six-story spine. The spine, if straightened, would be an intimidating 800 feet (250 meters) long. By articulating the plan into a blocky S shape, the architects divided the building into discrete wings, minimizing the apparent size of the building and allowing sunlight into all areas of the office. The folds of the new building frame four distinct roof terraces, each of which is designed to provide orientation and identity throughout the building.

An entry plaza moderates the grade change from the street to the building's main entry atop the parking garage roof. The northern half slopes gently, providing full accessibility, while feathered steps edge the northeast corner. The terrace is paved in dark gray, enlivened with Corten grates, scattered like confetti. Clumps of birches and circles of boxwood occupy Corten planters that are placed like raindrops on the terrace. The hedge planters are flush with the terrace surface; their soil volume is contained within the depth of the paving system. The trees, requiring greater soil volume, are set in raised planters; the thin steel edges rise approximately 18 inches (46 centimeters) above the terrace surface.

To the west, the folds of the new building enclose three additional green roof terraces: from south to north, a patio garden, a fern garden, and a parterre.

The section shows the slope of the entry plaza as it rises gently up to the plinth level. The parking beneath the entry continues under the new building wing.

ESSENT ROOFGARDENS

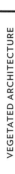
Some droplets have thin soils and low ground covers. Others use elegant weathered steel edging to contain deeper soils for trees.

**144**

The southernmost, a patio garden, is a minimalist wooden terrace providing seating and social space. The terrace uses the constraint of soil depth as a design opportunity. The perimeter of the terrace is planted in ground cover plants, which require only thin soils. The wooden patio is flush with the thin soils at the entrance doors; as it approaches the building's edge, it rises up with three low steps, subtly masking the planters thus created beneath its surface that contain enough soil to support a grove of honey locust. The elegant patio uses one constraint of green roofs as an opportunity to create subtle topographies.

The patio terrace is open to the west, so the honey locusts provide welcome shade from the afternoon sun; the trees buffer both the terrace and the offices inside the building. The shade garden to the north is enclosed on all sides, with a lower building wing to the east, so it has a very different microclimate—shady, cool, and calm. This central terrace uses the woods, and sylvan images, as its theme. Whole logs cut into segments are arranged in the shape of a fern frond, interplanted with birches and surrounded by ferns. The garden is a shady reminder of growth and decay. The dead logs will cover with moss and lichens; their strong pattern stands out year-round but especially in winter when most plants have died back and lost leaves. In the shade garden, the difficulty of green roof microclimates often being very different from the surrounding environment is turned to advantage through the use of shade-tolerant and evergreen plants, and the unusual use of logs and moss.

Finally, to the north is the baroque print garden, a visual mash-up of the baroque parterre and the high-tech printed circuit board. Boxwood lanes interlace with gravel paths and are accented by yews trimmed into neat cones. Spines of yellow

The shapes of the cut logs, interplanted with birches and framed with ferns, will slowly soften as mosses grow and the logs decompose.

145

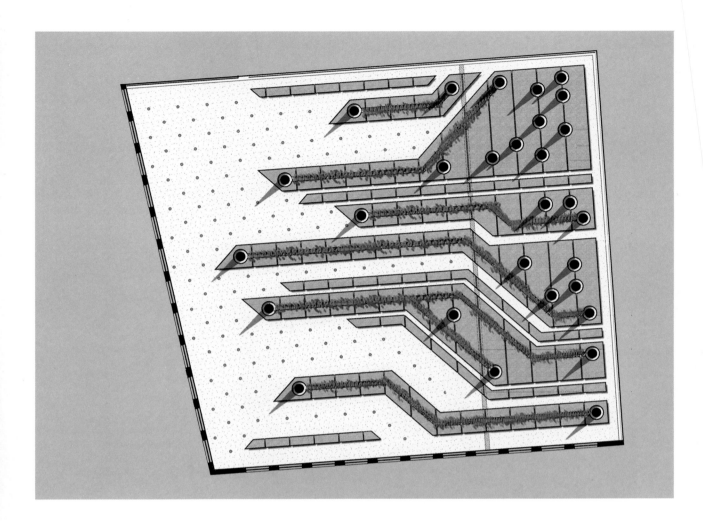

The print plaza was conceived as a tapis vert based on a high-tech form: the print board.

The fern garden, where logs are arranged in a frond shape, takes inspiration from the cool, shady setting.

VEGETATED ARCHITECTURE

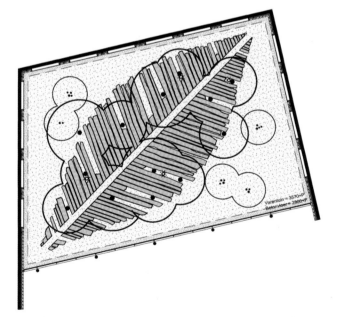

tulips send seasonal shots of energy and color down each boxwood lane. Extensive green roofs are, in some ways, little more than gravel-ballasted roofs in which plants are encouraged to grow. The print board parterre combines this reality with the historic precedent of gravel terraces, creating a playful and elegant garden in the sky.

At the Essent headquarters, green roofs are fully embraced as landscape architecture; they are treated as visual surfaces, technical opportunities, and sources of identity, orientation, and playful design. They are conceived and designed first as landscape rooms, with a social and representational program. The technical challenges of a garden above a building are taken as design opportunities: varied soil depths create spatial definition and topography; eccentric microclimates are highlighted as place-making opportunities; thin soils are embraced as gravel walks. The themes of each garden extend into the building: parterre, fern garden, and patio operate as points of orientation but also as neighborhood identities.

Low green and yellow plantings are accented with clipped yews.

**147**

# THE STORY OF
# WATER

## Our Water: An Interpretive Trail

This story starts in the Pacific Ocean and ends at your tap. The trail signs focus on the process of Metro Vancouver providing drinking water for the region. It circles the buildings and other structures that contains state-of-the-art water science and technology systems.

The trail signs also interpret many features of this amazing place, from how important sustainability is in every structure and process, to the value of geothermal energy, and wildlife habitat.

The Water Trail
Estimated length: 1 km
Elevation change: > 2 m
— The Water Trail
○ Barrier-free
■ Interpretive Features

Foot Bridge
Overflow Pond
Clearwell
You are here
Storm Water Pond
Seymour-Capilano Filtration Plant
Amphibian Pond
Public Parking

## What's Happening Here?

The buildings before you, and the ground under you, are all part of the process of providing drinking water. The plant is mixing, filtering and disinfecting the raw water from closed and protected reservoirs north and west of you. Below where you are standing, our water is ready to be sent to your city.

metrovancouver

Vegetated roof over a new
metropolitan water filtration plant,
creating native habitat and linking up
with the local recreational trail system

——

**VANCOUVER,
BRITISH COLUMBIA**

**DESIGNED BY**
Sharp & Diamond Landscape
Architecture Inc. (Vancouver,
British Columbia)

**COMPLETED IN 2010**

**6.2-ACRE VEGETATED ROOF ON
A 39.5-ACRE SITE, 25-ACRE SITE
RESTORATION / 2.5-HECTARE
VEGETATED ROOF ON A
16-HECTARE SITE, 10-HECTARE
SITE RESTORATION**

# SEYMOUR-CAPILANO FILTRATION PLANT

A living roof meadow fills
a critical niche in the surrounding forest ecosys-
tem. Interpretive signage
describes both the water
filtration process and the
green roof habitat.

——

**149**

Adjacent to the North Vancouver neighborhood of Lynn Valley,
6 acres (2.4 hectares) of lupines are blooming in a grassy meadow
scattered with logs and stumps. Grasses, shrubs, perennials, and
ferns thrive in the open site. It is a fairly typical scene in the Pacific
Northwest. Or it would be, if it weren't on top of a building—the
largest water filtration plant in Canada. The plant achieved a
LEED Gold rating by using a wide array of building and site
strategies to integrate into the local watershed and bioregion.

Porous paving in the parking area allows rainwater infiltration.

VEGETATED ARCHITECTURE

The Seymour-Capilano Filtration Plant is an ambitious project. The plant collects and treats water from two reservoirs (Seymour and Capilano) serving metro Vancouver. The reservoirs are connected via two 4.4-mile-long (7.1-kilometer-long) tunnels, excavated 525–2,100 feet (160–640 meters) below the ground. The plant's green design strategies include permeable paving in the parking lot; rain gardens to clean, cool, and infiltrate rain into the groundwater table; and thin-soil green roofs on the operations building (with a soil depth of 6–12 inches / 15–30 centimeters) planted in low-growing succulents and drought-tolerant grasses to clean, cool, and detain rainwater. Over the clear wells (large storage tanks that hold the water while it is being disinfected), an innovative vegetated roof restores not what used to be but what ought to be, ecologically speaking. Here, the filtration plant is treated as a human-created ecological disturbance, and the roof is designed as an early successional landscape.

Early successional landscapes serve critical ecological functions; in the Pacific Northwest, these meadows were historically created primarily by fire. In the region, lupines are among the first wildflowers to colonize a site after a disturbance such as a fire or a windstorm. Along with the slow decomposition of remaining woody debris—stumps and logs from trees killed in the disturbance—plants such as lupines help improve the soils on which Pacific Northwest forests grow. The biodiversity in these disturbed sites is astounding—mice and voles forage for grass seeds and nest in the downed wood; raptors watch from adjacent forests, preying on the rodents in the clearing. Bureau of Land Management research suggests that historically, these early successional meadows and shrublands were up to 35 percent of the Pacific Northwest landscape. Now, with the suppression of wildfires around timber forests and urban development, they are

Fir and maple seedlings are emerging among the restored rock and woody debris.

The meadow filled with lupines on the roof of the filtration plant and the surrounding forest perform important ecological functions for each other.

SEYMOUR-CAPILANO FILTRATION PLANT

as little as 2.5 percent of the region by some USDA Forest Service estimates. Loss of meadows puts not only meadow species at risk in a region but also the forest species that depend on them.

The vegetated roof was designed to serve three users: the environment, wildlife, and the public. Before construction began, a wildlife and habitat survey was completed for the entire 39.5-acre (16-hectare) site. Much of the site was restored to this surveyed preconstruction condition to the extent possible. However, it was determined that several key ecological pieces were missing in the region, including meadows. Sharp & Diamond designed the vegetated roof as a meadow ecosystem, to provide sunlight and wind-protected warmth for the plants and animals that thrive there. Early successional meadows are sites of extraordinary biodiversity, as plants and animals colonize the meadow and compete for dominance. As trees move in, biodiversity drops dramatically, only to increase again slowly over hundreds of years. Mature old-growth forests have levels of biodiversity similar to those found in early successional meadows. These mature forests can be five hundred or more years old, and they are, of course, composed of very different species from the early seral areas. Many of the old-growth forest species rely on other species found only in meadows.

The vegetated roof at Seymour-Capilano was designed to produce biodiversity. Before construction, plants, soil, rocks, logs, and stumps were collected on-site and stockpiled for use in the meadow. The native soil, plants, and animals are adapted to each other. The soil is rich in nutrients, insects and invertebrates, and fungi and bacteria that help native plants thrive and that feed animals low on the food chain such as birds and squirrels. The local plants—salal, mahonia, and ferns collected on-site, as well as meadow grasses and wildflowers introduced—provide food and nesting for animals. Stockpiled and reused rocks store heat; they collect sunlight and reradiate it at night into the soil and immediate air. Stumps and logs provide shelter for seedlings to grow and homes for small mammals and insects, as well as a pantry for the large mammals that feed on those insects. They slowly decompose and provide nutrients and water-storing organic material to the soil. Rocks and logs contain native mosses, lichens, and fungi, some of which can take decades to establish on a disturbed site. The vegetated roof, which is set into a slope and so is accessible at grade from two sides, is a complete meadow ecosystem, seeded with a complex web of organisms, and fills a necessary niche for the surrounding area.

The roof is huge—6.2 acres (2.5 hectares)—and the soils on it are extraordinarily heavy compared to most vegetated roofs. Rather than specifying a lightweight growth medium common on most green roofs, Sharp & Diamond reused the existing soil. And the soil is 40 inches (100 centimeters) deep, which allows large shrubs and even small trees to grow. The resulting weight of the roof solves an unusual problem that the clear wells within the building posed for the engineers. The clear wells are a final stage in the movement of water from natural stream and lake systems—where it may be contaminated with sediment, algae, or bacteria—to clean, potable municipal water. Depending on the process used and the size of the tanks, disinfection in the clear wells can take several days. While some stages of the filtration process can be open to the air, this near-final stage needs to occur sheltered from environmental contamination. And while the clear wells are filled

Woody debris provides habitat for insects, fungi, and other species that form a strong foundation for a food web. Metal hoods cover vents from the mechanical system, hinting at the expansive building below.

with water most of the time, they need to be emptied at times for maintenance and cleaning. They are so large, and the water weight so great, that when they are empty they can float, boatlike, in the groundwater table. The roof was designed to act as a weight holding down the entire building. The unusual program allowed an extraordinary vegetated roof with deep, heavy native soils.

But the roof is designed not only for animals and ecological services. The third user is the public, and the roof is open to the public and integrated into the extensive local trail system that links the most urban areas of North Vancouver with extraordinary natural reserves: canyons, mountains, waterfalls. The Seymour-Capilano plant sits between Lynn Canyon and Seymour River Canyon, each of which is crossed by bridges and trails; the filtration plant is near the Lower Seymour Conservation Reserve, which is designated a key node in the North Vancouver District trails system, a place where several major trails intersect. And it is approximately the halfway point of the eastern segment of the 30-mile (50-kilometer) Baden-Powell Trail, a popular trail that runs east-west across the entire peninsula. By integrating the plant into the urban trail network, Sharp & Diamond has created a pleasant addition to the hikes, with a very different aesthetic and experience from the surrounding woods. The landscape architects have also created an educational site where visitors can learn about the demands of gathering and supplying municipal water, as well as about the regional ecosystem and the relationship between iconic forests and meadows.

The Seymour-Capilano vegetated roof is one of only a handful of vegetated roofs designed to fully integrate into its local ecosystem. And it pushes that vision perhaps farther than any other similar project. In part, this is due to the unusual program, which allowed massive weight on the roof. The designers were able to

Visitors can access the roof from the network of paths and trails in the area.

VEGETATED ARCHITECTURE

take the engineering problem of anchoring the building to the ground and turn it into a design opportunity. The early integration of wildlife biologists and ecologists gave the designers a rich understanding of the ecological context of the project and also gave them access to emerging ecological research on succession and the importance of native soils and woody debris in habitat creation. And while many vegetated roofs are closed to the public, this one is fully integrated into the urban recreation system. This decision by Vancouver Metro and the water agency lets the project be more than an inaccessible building tactic. Instead, it is a place of recreation, enjoyment, and education.

Lupines, a common early successional species, were planted to add color and also improve the soils.

# ECOLOGICAL URBANISM

## Design Informed by Natural Systems

Kokkedal Climate
Adaptation Plan in
Kokkedal, Denmark.

**IN TESTIMONY TO A** U.S. Senate subcommittee on forest and public lands management in which she advocated for wilderness designation of 5.7 million acres (2.3 million hectares) of federal lands in Utah, writer Terry Tempest Williams said, "What do we wish for? To be whole. To be complete. Wildness reminds us what it means to be human, what we are connected to rather than what we are separate from." Parks and plazas, gardens and lawns—works of landscape architecture are inherently part of living systems. Regardless of the designer's intent, these places are embedded in and alter natural systems. They direct, channel, and pool water; they provide habitat for plants and animals, and for the human animal. They are places for connection to the seasonal and diurnal patterns of a region, and to the ever-shifting, ever-predictable patterns of water, wind, light. Ecological systems are at the core of landscape architecture, and increasingly, designers are returning to them as a source of inspiration and creativity.

Natural systems are a fundamental preoccupation of landscape architects. It was only in the industrial era, and especially the twentieth century, that designers proposed an art-for-art's-sake approach to landscape design, uncoupled from the contingencies of soil and biota. Before that uncoupling, Frederick Law Olmsted proposed many of his works as informed by and integrated into natural systems, from the geomorphically derived Prospect Park to the reconstructed wetlands of Boston's Back Bay Fens. And even at the height of twentieth-century modernism, Ian McHarg reminded designers to study landscape systems prior to design in order to determine the site's suitability to support different programs, both cultural and natural. Olmsted and his contemporaries were early moderns, calling for more interdisciplinary work even as design and engineering professions evolved into discrete nodes of expertise.

Eighty years later, McHarg and his peers were responding to an environmental crisis caused, in part, by that professionalization—the impacts of one technical decision seen and monitored only in another field. McHarg's analytical overlays were a physical metaphor of the need in the design professions to reintegrate synthetic and multivalent thinking. The context of landscape design has shifted, both culturally and physically. Global networks of employment, production, and consumption foster disconnection from the physical and living places we occupy. And an unprecedented shift in climate, with predictions (and early indications) of devastating impacts, forces us to consider, as Tempest Williams did, what we wish for. How do we resist, accommodate, and adapt to these shifts? Jane Amidon, director of the Urban Landscape Program at Northeastern University, suggests that we are entering a new era of environmentalism, one where stewardship of the environment is defined through "an entrepreneurial redefinition of our relationship to nature."

That redefinition is being hypothesized, in part, through design. Landscape architects are plumbing the depths of sites—underlying geology, soils, and hydrology; occupying flora and fauna; animating sun, wind, and rain—to inform designs that perform intentionally, ecologically. Ecological design thinking operates in at least three ways: through considerations of form, scale, and social impact.

When considering ecological form, designers analyze the existing and potential flow of water, nutrients, flora, and fauna on a site, and design to accommodate those life processes. Ecologist Chris Maser describes ecological systems as having composition, structure, and function—that is, elements within a system, their physical arrangement, and the processes, actions, or relationships that arrangement facilitates. Ecological design requires all three of these considerations: what, where, and why. The projects in this chapter design with or for specific species of plants and animals, arranged in intentional patterns, to effect desired results.

Considerations of scale recognize that a project is situated within, and contains within it, nested systems. The scale of inquiry, whether a courtyard, a park, or an urban district, is always embedded within a more expansive scale; actions taken on a site extend out into the region. These projects recognize the extension of a design beyond its own physical and temporal boundaries. They are not predicated on a static view of an aesthetic site but rather conceive of design as a locus for relationships and changes over space and time.

Considerations of social impact acknowledge that ecological design is not just about ecology itself. It is also, as Amidon posits, about questioning and redefining our understanding of ecology. It provides a point of connection between natural and cultural systems—a point where, perhaps, critique can occur. At its simplest, ecological design can be affective, providing beneficial habitat for the human animal and a range of health benefits including empathy, stress relief, and a bolstered immune system. But perhaps this recognition that we are part of the ecosystem, that the dyad of nature and culture is reductive and not terribly helpful, suggests that ecological design is also critical and self-reflective, and can be a source of redefinition and stewardship.

Two of the projects that follow operate in this critical, affective realm. Teardrop Park is a representation of ecosystem components that provides access to the forms and experiences of nature. The forms are the tinder, the experiences a spark for igniting a land ethic. Péage Sauvage, in contrast, is an uncrossable threshold to a fragile ecosystem, providing a sense of awe and humility in the face of nature's implacable resilience.

Teardrop Park draws on the geomorphology and plant communities of the Catskills for its composition, and on the microclimate and hydrology of the site for its structure. The result is a park that operates as a map garden or arboretum of the larger bioregion, connecting urban residents to the larger landscape through sensory experience of plants and stone. And by avoiding typical park structures in favor of rock climbing walls and slopes and winding gravel paths, the park creates the experiences of a natural setting—the sense of undirected exploration, the ability to get lost (even briefly) in a grove. This presentation of the bioregion, and of natural experience, provides an affective point of connection for residents, especially children, and perhaps helps to foster a sense of connectedness and stewardship.

Péage Sauvage, in Nantes, France, is nearly an inversion of Teardrop Park. Here "real" nature is presented, but access and interaction with that nature is highly limited. The project provides a gathering place for social and educational activities, adjacent to what Gilles Clément calls a third landscape—a fecund ruderal landscape that has emerged from a bombed and abandoned urban site. The nature reserve, the Petite Amazonie, is inaccessible to most, and a plaza provides a viewpoint for peering into the edges of the off-limits ecosystem. Where Teardrop Park provides physical, sensory experiences as a springboard for exploration and understanding, Péage Sauvage provides mystery and separation, creating a sense of respect for the fragile tenacity of natural systems. Both projects ask us to question our relationship to nature—whether to engage more or to step back in awe and wonder.

Two projects explore the integration of natural systems into urban contexts, and the social, ecological, and formal opportunities that provides. They reorient cities to lost or hidden natural systems and morphologies that organized and oriented the sites before human settlement. Buffalo Bayou, in Houston, Texas, uses the technical problem of mitigating urban flooding as an opportunity for improved ecological and social structure and function, hybridizing natural and cultural functions. By regrading the banks of the bayou, the designers increased flood storage and physical and visual access to the waterway, and also slowed the floodwater, which helps to filter and settle sediment and reduce erosion, all of which improves water quality. And through thoughtful clearing and replanting, the flora of the park now protects the slope from erosion, filters floodwater, and provides nesting and foraging habitat for native species. While reducing flooding, the designers also created an extraordinary urban and ecological amenity for the majority of days when the bayou is not in flood.

At Wijkeroogpark, in Velsen-Noord, the Netherlands, the function of a brackish stream was restored in a completely altered form. Like Buffalo Bayou, the Scheybeeck Stream was restored to ecological function: designers daylighted a piped stream, recreated a brackish marsh, and allowed periodic flooding into new marshes. But unlike Buffalo Bayou, the new form of the Scheybeeck is highly artificial and clearly an act of design. The composition and function restore the natural system, but the structure is clearly cultural.

Finally, a new neighborhood plan for Kokkedal, a town north of Copenhagen, prepares the city for changes in its environmental and ecological context. The urban plan intends to make the city resilient in the face of climate change. In Kokkedal, climate change models predict more frequent, intense rainstorms, with associated flooding of urban streams and storm sewer systems. The Kokkedal plan accommodates that predicted flooding in an urban network of channels and flood storage areas that operate, primarily, as urban amenities—verdant streets and basinlike recreation areas.

Discussing psychotherapist and philosopher Félix Guattari's call to reconsider the impact of human action on ecosystems, and the ethics and modes of cultural production, architect and educator Mohsen Mostafavi has suggested an "ecological design practice that does not simply take account of the fragility of the ecosystem and the limits on resources but considers such conditions the essential basis for a new form of creative imagining." This practice, inspired by the constraints and internal logic of natural processes at a variety of temporal and spatial scales, weaves through the projects that follow, and through many of the projects in other chapters as well. In response to external pressures of resource depletion and climate change, landscape architects are looking internally—to the site itself, to ecological and systems theories—to inform designs that question and critique our production of sites and our relation to the sites themselves.

Péage Sauvage, in Nantes, France: The plaza is a threshold to an urban wilderness that has grown in the city.

The structure draws on the forms of an unbuilt highway, repurposing them from an infrastructure of speed and distance to one of slowness and connection.

163

DESIGN INFORMED BY NATURAL SYSTEMS

**Urban courtyard park with lawn, amphitheater, and sand and water play areas**

———

**NEW YORK, NEW YORK**

**DESIGNED BY**
Michael Van Valkenburgh Associates, Inc. (Brooklyn, New York)

**COMPLETED IN 2006**
(north park)

**2010**
(south park)

**2.3 ACRES**
(1.8 acres, north; 0.5 acres, south)

**0.93 HECTARES**
(0.73 hectares, north; 0.2 hectares, south)

# TEARDROP PARK

Throughout the park, walls are tactile and inviting.

The design encourages visitors, especially children, to immerse themselves in natural textures and sounds, to experience uneven footing, and to challenge gravity.

———

**165**

Teardrop Park is a walk in the woods in a city where nature can be difficult to access. The park provides a shadbush knoll, a beech grove, a marsh, a witch hazel dell, and other ecological communities, as well as outcrops and geologic formations that provide opportunities for learning through engagement with the park. And by providing the experiences of nature—uneven footing, rocky climbing areas, winding brambles—the park provides opportunities for urban children to reap the benefits of play in nature.

For most children in New York, parks consist of hardscape, play equipment, sandboxes, and perhaps some water play. While the city's large parks offer woods, streams, and marshes, opportunities to explore those areas can be limited. In both Prospect and Central parks, the wilder areas are often fenced off, both to protect the natural reserves and for human security. At Teardrop Park, Battery Park City Authority (BPCA) wanted to create a place where visitors, especially the children in the neighborhood, could experience a walk in the Catskills—both the forms of woods, ravines, outcrops, and watercourses, and the experiences of undirected exploration and discovery.

The park continues a line of inquiry that includes Frederick Law Olmsted and Lawrence Halprin, that Halprin termed *experiential equivalency*—recreating the physical and emotional experience of a place without trying to recreate the place itself. Teardrop Park, like Olmsted's Central Park or Halprin's Freeway Park, integrates into ecological systems as a side effect of being a planted space in a city. But the primary functions of these parks are cultural. They are meant to stimulate visitors, to provide the sensory and emotional phenomena of natural settings, and to provide educational opportunities so visitors can learn about the natural systems of a city and its surrounding environment.

When developing the northern edge of Battery Park City, the BPCA decided to combine the open space for four residential towers. Rather than four small, private courtyards divided by an intersection, the four towers face onto a large, shared, public park. Then-BPCA president and CEO Tim Carey wanted the park to

The microclimate diagram shows the passive program elements located in the northern, sunnier half and the more active program elements located in the deep shade to the south.

ECOLOGICAL URBANISM

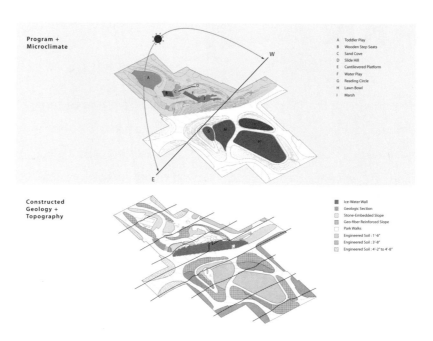

Program + Microclimate

A   Toddler Play
B   Wooden Step Seats
C   Sand Cove
D   Slide Hill
E   Cantilevered Platform
F   Water Play
G   Reading Circle
H   Lawn Bowl
I   Marsh

Constructed Geology + Topography

Ice-Water Wall
Geologic Section
Stone-Embedded Slope
Geo-fiber Reinforced Slope
Park Walks
Engineered Soil : 1'-6"
Engineered Soil : 3'-8"
Engineered Soil : 4'-2" to 4'-8"

feel like a walk in the Catskills and selected Michael Van Valkenburgh Associates (MVVA) to create that vision. In addition to the design constraint of providing a naturalistic experience in the city, the designers were also confronted with serious site constraints. Topography, water, sun, and wind combined to make a harsh and rather dull site. The area was completely flat, created land, a landfill along the Hudson River from the original construction of the World Trade Center in the 1980s. The site has a high water table, and saline water from the river moves onto the site subsurficially. As a result, soils for planting were not deep. The towers, between 210 and 235 feet (64 and 72 meters) tall, would cast long shadows on the park for much of the day, making many areas cold and difficult to plant. And the park is very close to the Hudson River and is subjected to fierce winds at times, channeled between the two western towers. These environmental conditions, which could have been constraints, were used instead as the park's ordering system.

MVVA used topography to create the desired experience of exploration, of climbing hills and descending ravines, of sheltered glens, and in the process also solved the technical problems of poor soil, solar and wind constraints, and a high water table. The designers organized spaces so that the active areas, likely to be used in summer, are to the south, kept shaded and cool for active recreation. Calmer uses are located to the north, in the sun. An oval lawn provides space for relaxing; by raising the north edge of the lawn, the designers maximized its solar exposure. MVVA designed the rolling topography to buffer certain areas, such as the lawn, from the punishing winds, while channeling winds through other, more active areas. The attention to microclimate is evident on the harshest days: in cooler weather, the lawn is quite popular, as are dark stones that soak up sunlight and reradiate warmth, while on hot summer days, the southern play areas are full of children, parents, and passers-by enjoying the shade, the breezes, and the water play areas. The topography also provides deeper soils to support lush planting, although tall trees

Signage throughout the park provides ecological information on species and ecotypes.

The lawn receives more sun than other areas of the park, with the added benefit of light reflected off the eastern building in the afternoon.

are notably absent, which hints at the hidden site beneath the surface. Even with the created hills, the water table is too high to support large trees.

Teardrop Park is an ecological laboratory for all ages. Young children can use the entire park as a playground, exploring plants, water, and sand and reaping the benefits of nature play. Older visitors can explore eleven distinct districts, and through signage and plant tags, learn about horticulture and ecological communities. From play to plant communities, the park offers a number of opportunities for environmental engagement and education. Perhaps most significant is the impact on young children. A wide range of research has shown the benefits of nature play for children: preventing or reducing obesity; increasing health and resistance to illness such as asthma; increasing attention and focus; decreasing stress and depression. To see these benefits, children not only need outdoor play time; they need play time in settings with natural qualities.

Judith Heerwagen has identified six qualities of natural settings, and their benefits. First, Heraclitean movement—patterns that are constantly changing in a predictable way (like cloud patterns, dappled sunlight in woods, or ripples in water)—stimulate the imagination while also calming and relieving stress. Second, temporal change, over days or seasons, affirms life processes while modeling growth and resiliency as a response to stress. Third, "rhyming" forms (similar yet different patterns and structures, such as the variability in the leaves of a plant); fourth, complexity; and fifth, multisensory experiences, stimulate curiosity, exploration, and appreciation, as well as lay the foundation for rational functions of distinguishing and classifying types. And sixth, unstructured play, rather than equipment with only one use, allows children to transform their environment, providing an outlet for creativity as well as a sense of control and ownership of space, fostering empowerment. Providing children access to sunlight, plants, and water also provides them with a range of experiences that relax, empower, engage, and expand.

At Teardrop Park, MVVA worked with nature play expert Robin Moore to design the entire park as a playground. There is no equipment, other than a slide that sits on a rocky slope. Instead, children manipulate the plants, water, and sand of the park. In a sand area, children control the amount of water spilling from a pump onto a rock basin and then into the sand, while square wooden platforms around the sand provide comfortable seating for adults as well as a place for children to jump and balance, or quietly observe other children. In a rocky outcrop area, the custom-built slide sits on the slope. Children clamber up the boulders to either side, finding their own path to the top. Water play rocks, an ice rock wall, and a marsh provide places where children can explore and alter their environment, while a reading circle and lawn provide areas for calm relaxation.

Through play, children experience the qualities of different kinds of rock, of water, of different types of leaves.

Stone stairs, boulders, and cobbles allow children to explore the different properties of stone en route to the slide.

**Building Entry**
Redbud
Meserve Holly
Korean Spicebush Viburnum
Fothergilla
Hosta
Daylily
Narcissus

**Boulder Slope**
Hornbeam, Hop Hornbeam
Oakleaf Hydrangea
Swamp Azalea
Ferns [Maiden Hair, Wood, Christmas]
False Solomon's Seal
Solomon's Seal
Redbud

**Shadbush Knoll**
Shadbush
Red Chokecherry
Downy Serviceberry
Shadbush
Narcissus
Siberian Squill
Yellowroot
Vinca

**South Entry**
River Birch
Goldenrain Tree
Arrowwood Viburnum
Linden Viburnum
Spring Witch Hazel
Inkberry
Black Snake Root
Daylily
Wood Anemone
Intermediate Wood Fern

**Marsh**
Highbush Blueberry
Inkberry
Winterberry
Tupelo
Summersweet
Joe Pye Weed
Swamp Milkweed
Blue Flag Iris
Sensitive Fern
Royal Fern
Cinnamon Fern
Interrupted Fern

**Ice Wall Crown**
Sumac
Burkwood Viburnum
Virginia Creeper
Smoke Bush
New England Aster
Cranberry Viburnum

**North Slope**
Pin Oak
American Holly
Winter Hazel
Inkberry
Hay-scented Fern
Christmas Fern
Wood Fern
Spanish Bluebells

**Witch Hazel Dell**
Spring Witch Hazel
Autumn Witch Hazel
Swamp Azalea
Intermediate Wood Fern
Wood Fern
Spiderwort
Forget-Me-Not

**Beech Grove**
American Beech
European Hornbeam
Carolina Silverbells
Fothergilla
Wild Sweet William
Wood Fern
Wake Robin
Pennsylvania Sedge

**Hellebore Hill**
Hellebore
Carolina Silverbell
Redbud
Ferns [Goldie's Wood, Sensitive]
Lady's-Slippper
Virginia Sweetspire
Swamp Azalea
Oakleaf Hydrangea

**Lawn**
Tall Fescue
[Grande, Coronado,
and Matador cultivars]

Crocus
Glory Of The Snow
Siberian Squill

*labels on diagram:* semi-shade, deep shade, dry, windy, sunny, shaded, from site runoff, dry, partial sun, partial sun, 2:1 steep slope, partial sun, protected, dry

The axonometric diagram shows the eleven planting zones. Plants were selected for their decorative and educational qualities, as well as for the beneficial habitat they provide.

ECOLOGICAL URBANISM

The relatively small park contains eleven distinct zones, each with its own microclimate of shade, water, and wind. MVVA took advantage of this difficult site and calibrated the plant communities to the various microclimates. The designers worked with ecologists to engineer organic soils to support each plant community, which are primarily native plants. Through soil design for drainage, compaction, and nutrient needs, and postinstallation soil monitoring and application of compost teas, 99.5 percent of the park's more than three thousand trees and shrubs have survived without herbicides, pesticides, or fungicides.

The plant palette is unusual for an urban park. Dense shade from the surrounding buildings and a high water table constrained the planting options, as did the desire to use primarily native plants. While building entries have decorative plants such as redbud, viburnum, fothergilla, and daylilies, the majority of the planting has a more subtle beauty than typical urban plants. A shadbush knoll, a marsh, a beech grove, a witch hazel dell, and the ice wall crown—planted in sumac, viburnum, aster, and Virginia creeper—provide a complex environment where 88 percent of the trees, shrubs, and perennials are native to the region. Bluestone walls and sandstone boulders are formed from stone quarried within 160 miles (257 kilometers) of the park. The mix of Hudson River Valley landscapes—lawns, hills, wetlands, forests—and the rich mix of plants stimulates the senses and rewards deeper inquiry with lessons about native plants and plant communities. While not explicitly didactic, the park fosters environmental education and stewardship through sensory engagement and delight.

The designers of Teardrop Park did not intend it to be a natural reserve or an ecological restoration project. But while it is important to design environments that integrate into local ecosystems, it is also important to design places that foster appreciation and stewardship of those environments. Especially in our largest cities, "natural" or "ecological" may not mean a reserve focused on nonhuman animals. Through Halprin's concept of experiential equivalences, we can provide habitat for the human animal that also forms bonds of appreciation, understanding, and stewardship with native ecosystems. In the process, Teardrop Park has also proved very successful as a site for migratory birds, as the native plants provide much-needed food and shelter in the city. Stephen J. Gould said, "We cannot win this battle to save species and environments without forging an emotional bond between ourselves and nature as well—for we will not fight to save what we do not love." At Teardrop Park, children and adults are given the opportunity to forge that emotional bond with a complex, diverse, engaging environment.

The rock wall is a source of delight for children and adults, and a popular climbing location.

**Public art and open space, incorporating a pavilion and a lawn, adjacent to a nature reserve**

———

**NANTES, FRANCE**

**DESIGNED BY**
Observatorium
(Rotterdam, the Netherlands)

**COMPLETED IN 2012**

**1 ACRE / 0.4 HECTARE**

# PÉAGE SAUVAGE

The park uses the forms of an unbuilt roadway as a vantage point into a nature preserve.

———

**173**

In a clearing in the woods stands a line of five wooden tollbooths. Wooden lanes sweep up to the booths and stop. Beyond, the earth rises in a slope, an impenetrable mass of vegetation; to either side, wooden on- and off-ramps lead toward vernal pools, then abruptly end. A clearing surrounds the tollbooths, but you sense that the surrounding trees and shrubs are beginning to claim the meadow, inch by inch. This dreamlike clearing feels like a place in a fairy tale, a frozen moment, an incomplete project, with materials transformed and the sleeping site slowly becoming overgrown.

Péage Sauvage, the Wilderness Tollbooth, is part park, part sculpture. The enigmatic structure stands at the threshold between the city of Nantes and an urban wilderness—the Petite Amazonie—that has grown in since World War II. The project draws on the history of the site and the tensions revealed in that history. It is a site formed by the most advanced technology—airplanes, bombs, highways—and by the slow, steady action of ecological colonization. In the past, this area of marshes and creeks was ignored or treated as a blank field for urban development and infrastructure. Riddled with craters after heavy bombing during World War II, the site was slated for development as part of a ring road system. Now, the sculptural tollbooths draw you to the edge of a nature reserve but don't allow you to pass through to the stream beyond; the structure is simultaneously a threshold to wilderness and a barrier, highlighting the need for cities sometimes to simply let nature run its own uninterrupted course.

The Petite Amazonie is a strange site, one that questions our assumptions about the relationship of nature and culture, and the modern myth of the forward march

The wooden tollbooths provide a platform for looking into the inaccessible marshes and forest beyond.

———

Péage Sauvage is an enigmatic design—part sculpture, part plaza, and threshold to a nature reserve with highly limited access.

of technology. The area is bounded by the sweeping curves of rail lines, adjacent to the Nantes train station. This important infrastructure was heavily bombed in World War II. British and American air raids on the railroads in German-occupied Nantes during the spring and summer of 1944 left swaths of land cratered and in ruins. While other blocks were rebuilt, the area bounded by rail lines lay fallow until the 1970s, when the city planned a massive highway through Nantes that would cross the site. The project was initiated: gravel extracted from another construction project was used to create embankments in the area. But there was a great deal of conflict about the impact the highway would have on the town, and eventually the project was abandoned and the area remained undeveloped. For nearly seventy years after World War II, the area was slowly reclaimed by nature;

bomb craters filled with water and mud, and woods grew up around the marshy center. The site became what landscape architect Gilles Clément calls a third landscape—a landscape left to its own processes that is spatially undetermined and often rich in biodiversity and genetic reserves. Writes Clément, "The Third Landscape . . . designates the sum of the space left over by man to landscape evolution—to nature alone. . . . Compared to the territories submitted to the control and exploitation by man, the Third Landscape forms a privileged area of receptivity to biological diversity."

The area became known as the Petite Amazonie, the Little Amazon. It is approximately 60 acres (24 hectares) of lush growth, centered on a stream and pond network, with areas of ash, willow, and alder woods along with meadow and wetlands.

Extensive wildlife includes waterbirds and songbirds, reptiles and amphibians, and mammals, including some nationally protected species. In 2004, the Petite Amazonie was designated part of the Natura 2000 network of more than 27,000 natural sites throughout Europe, the first urban natural space with that designation. Natura 2000 has two designations of sites: Special Protection Areas (SPAs), to protect habitat for endangered bird species, and the more restrictive Special Areas of Conservation (SACs), to preserve rare and endangered animals, plants, and habitats. The Petite Amazonie is part of the Loire Estuary Natura 2000 site and has both SPA and SAC designation, a testament to its extraordinary qualities. To protect the area, access is highly limited; only three hundred people per year are allowed on tours of the reserve, organized by the French League for Bird Protection (LPO).

Because of the history of this site, the simple presence of woods, meadow, and marsh is a manifesto on how tenuous our control of nature ever is. Rail lines severed the marshes from the tidal Loire River; airplanes and bombs permanently altered the topography and destroyed much of Nantes; the imagined highway would have divided the city and cut it off from its river. But the natural processes of the site slowly, implacably continued as soon as planning stepped aside. The intellectual capacity used in attempts to plan and control this landscape is staggering, as is the futility of those attempts.

The LPO wanted a place for citizens to engage with the Petite Amazonie, and in 2010, with Estuaire artistic director, David Moinard, co-commissioned Observatorium, an artist collective from Rotterdam, to design a site-specific work there

The Petite Amazonie is a "third landscape"—an overlooked site in the heart of the city that has grown, largely through neglect, into a site rich in biodiversity.

_____

A preliminary design sketch shows the ramps and tollbooths stopping at the edge of the reserve, expressing the frustrated desire to control the site through technology.

as part of Estuaire 2012. Over three seasons, this public arts program has created an art trail along the Loire River between Nantes and Saint-Nazaire to reveal the ecological and industrial heritage of the Loire estuary. The 30-mile (48-kilometer) trail links the two cities, and its twenty-two works of art, installation, and design highlight particular sites and landscapes along the estuary. The broad, short estuary is a significant migratory flyway for waterbirds, and its mudflats, reed beds, and marshes provide a range of ecological functions. More than 37,000 acres (15,000 hectares) have been set aside within the estuary as part of the Natura 2000 network.

Péage Sauvage highlights the Petite Amazonie as a unique site within the estuary. And it tells the story of a site that operates as a reminder of the futility of attempting to control natural processes. The tollbooths and roadways trace the path of the unbuilt highway, but they are transformed into a plaza, benches, and a viewing platform for peering into the forbidden jungle. The upper deck of the tollbooth is open daily, and the LPO uses the site as a meeting point and a viewpoint into the nature reserve. And the project will unfold over time; the vegetation of the nature reserve will be allowed to slowly expand and completely encircle the clearing and the structure.

The strange and abrupt object, with its domestic material and industrial scale, and its obviously truncated forms, stands in contrast to the spatially vague wetlands around it. This material and spatial contrast focuses the visitor's attention on the ecology of the site. Rather than attempting to integrate ecology into the city, Péage Sauvage simply leaves it alone and provides a threshold into a place with a different set of processes. Residents of the adjacent Malakoff neighborhood helped to create links between the community and the artwork through publications, educational programming, and play.

The designers at Observatorium explain the project through a fable published in Malakoff's community newsletter, *Malacocktail*. "A Fable of Progress, Conflict, a Swamp, and Three Craftsmen" is a fairy tale telling of the destruction and growth of the Petite Amazonie, and three foreign craftsmen who make a place for trees, animals, and people to meet. The eldest craftsman hears the voice of an oak tree sighing, "I hear people calling this the Petite Amazonie. My feet have been in this swamp for 40 years. New trees and plants keep coming and our clever little jungle grows not only in water but also on concrete. . . . Our brothers and sisters around the city are fertilized, cropped and cuddled the whole time—that is no good. We are happy here as we are. We can take care of ourselves. But a little more company would be nice, don't you agree?" Péage Sauvage lets the trees continue to take care of themselves but provides a little company, for the swamp and for the city.

Visitors gather on the ramps and tollbooths.

**179**

PÉAGE SAUVAGE

**Linear park providing flood control and ecological restoration along with jogging and biking trails**

———

**HOUSTON, TEXAS**

**DESIGNED BY**
SWA Group (Houston)

**COMPLETED IN 2006**

**23 ACRES, 1.2 MILES /
9.3 HECTARES, 1.9 KILOMETERS**

# BUFFALO BAYOU PROMENADE

The floodway acts as a park most days of the year, and a new pedestrian bridge connects the two sides of the bayou.

Buffalo Bayou Promenade solves technical problems of flooding while also improving ecological structure and function, and providing Houstonians with access to their waterfront.

———

In the middle of downtown Houston, an alligator is floating down a bayou, lazily drifting in the muddy current. A group of park visitors excitedly points out its snout, the ridges on its back. On any given day, Houstonians can see three kinds of turtles, heron, osprey, songbirds, a colony of 150,000 bats, and even the reclusive alligator sunning on the silty banks in the middle of the fourth-largest city in the United States. This is an astonishing reversal for a bayou that until fairly recently was inhospitable to people as well as animals—a foul, polluted channel filled with trash.

Buffalo Bayou, apparently named for the bison that once roamed this landscape, is Houston's generative force. The city was developed in 1836 at the confluence of Buffalo and White Oak bayous, and the urban grid was laid out parallel to a reach of Buffalo Bayou. The waterway served as the city's primary transportation and shipping infrastructure, and by the early twentieth century, the channel had been dredged from 9 feet (2.7 meters) deep to 25 feet (7.6 meters) deep to allow oceangoing boats access to the port. But while urban access to water was good for transport, it was a problem in storms: the tidal bayou, waterway for a 102-square-mile (264-square-kilometer) watershed, was prone to flooding. Following devastating floods in 1929 and 1935, the Army Corps of Engineers designed a flood-control plan for the bayou. By the 1960s, the Corps had built an upstream dam and reservoir to control inflow to the bayou and had channelized White Oak Bayou, removing riparian vegetation and straightening its meanders. Concerned by White Oak Bayou's transformation into a concrete channel, Houstonians rallied to protect Buffalo Bayou and to preserve the urban ecosystem.

A 2002 master plan by Thompson Design Group set the framework for hybrid improvement to the floodwater infrastructure that also improved the bayou's ecological function. The master plan refocused the city around the bayou, provided access for recreation and social events, and used the green infrastructure as a catalyst for economic development. The plan conceptually divided the bayou into three zones—a downtown sector flanked by more expansive, meandering, and wild east and west sectors. The plan envisioned green fingers reaching into downtown Houston, pedestrian areas that would include street plantings to provide visibility and access to the bayou and also to slow, clean, and cool storm water before it entered the bayou.

Lower-elevation paths, whose locations were constrained by the overhead highways, can get covered in thick mud.

A vibrant program of events ensures that Houstonians are getting back to the bayou.

———

Buffalo Bayou has a 102-square-mile (264-square-kilometer) watershed, most of which flows through downtown Houston.

ECOLOGICAL URBANISM

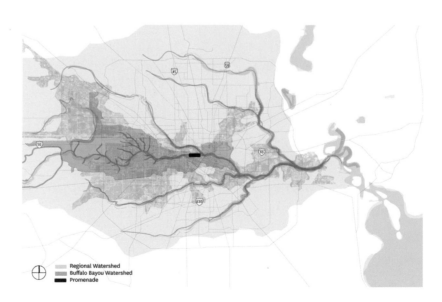

Regional Watershed
Buffalo Bayou Watershed
Promenade

The redesigned edge disperses the energy of floods and filters floodwater. Gabion retaining walls slow the water, a riparian edge of Mexican petunia and Louisiana iris filters smaller debris, and a tree layer traps larger debris.

———

The site plan shows broad swaths of plantings that respond to the different constraints: floodwater, erosion, overhead highways. The structural complexity of ground covers, shrub layer, understory, and canopy—largely native species—improves the habitat value of the bayou.

This section dramatically shows how much soil was removed. The new grading provides greater flood storage capacity, and the gentler slopes allow views into the park, increasing both the presence of the bayou and the safety of the park.

**184**

Buffalo Bayou Promenade reclaims the downtown sector, serving as an ecological and urban amenity. Before the project, the bayou was largely inaccessible to Houstonians, with limited entry points and steep 20-to-30-foot (6-to-9-meter) banks. It felt unsafe, with limited visibility into the bayou. About 40 percent of the promenade is covered by freeway infrastructure—on-ramps, bridges, overpasses—which creates shaded nooks that added to the sense of danger. It was also inhospitable to wildlife. Trash collected in the bayou, trapped against bridge piers and among overgrown invasive shrubs. Fast-moving floodwater eroded the banks, and the silt removed from the banks clogged the water. The bayou had the worst water quality of any Texas stream or river and was nearly intolerable to aquatic species. To restore the bayou's ecological function and turn it into an attractive urban park would require considerable ingenuity.

SWA Group faced extreme challenges at Buffalo Bayou: steep slopes, eroded banks, overhead infrastructure, invasive plants, limited access, and extremely poor water quality. The promenade at first glance is a successful urban park, 23 acres (9.3 hectares) of open space and jogging and biking trails, with beautiful planting, lush shade, and lovely views of the bayou and the skyline. But the promenade is more than just a park; it also functions as a flood control mechanism, an ecological restoration, and an urban amenity. It is part of a growing movement in landscape infrastructure benefiting from hybrid cultural and ecological spaces. Rather than addressing flooding with a narrow, straight, steep channel that moves water quickly out of an urban center, landscape infrastructures disperse and slow water, spreading storm water both spatially and temporally. Wenk Associates' Shop Creek in Denver was an early example of using wetlands and stream meanders to slow water, wetlands to filter sediment and pollution, and deep pools to settle

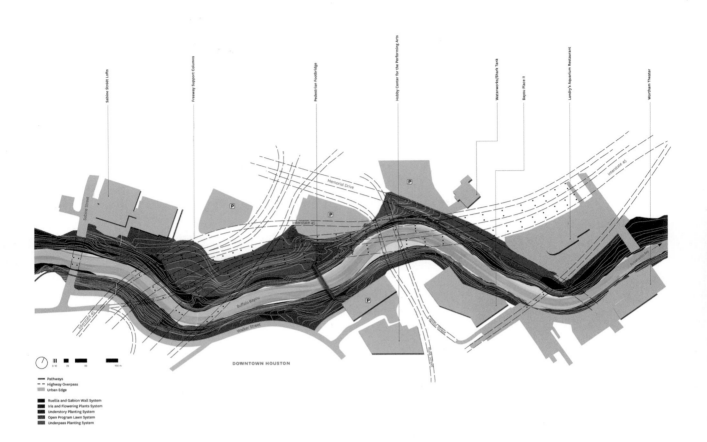

Sabine Street Lofts
Freeway Support Columns
Pedestrian Footbridge
Hobby Center for the Performing Arts
Waterworks/Shark Tank
Bayou Place II
Landry's Aquarium Restaurant
Wortham Theater

Memorial Drive
Interstate 45
Buffalo Bayou
Walker Street
Sabine Street

DOWNTOWN HOUSTON

Pathways
Highway Overpass
Urban Edge

Ruellia and Gabion Wall System
Iris and Flowering Plants System
Understory Planting System
Open Program Lawn System
Underpass Planting System

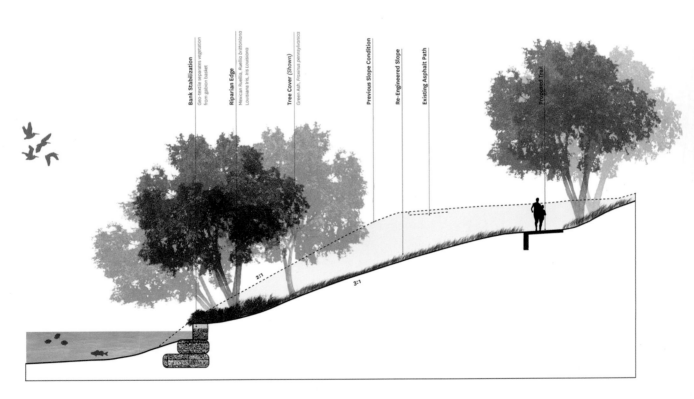

**Bank Stabilization**
Geo-textile separates vegetation from gabion basket

**Riparian Edge**
Mexican Ruellia, *Ruellia brittoniana*
Louisiana Iris, *Iris Louisiana*

**Tree Cover (Shown)**
Green Ash, *Fraxinus pennsylvanica*

**Previous Slope Condition**

**Re-Engineered Slope**

**Existing Asphalt Path**

**Proposed Trail**

2:1

3:1

sediment out of the creek's water. The approach is becoming more common, but Buffalo Bayou Promenade is one of the largest and most urban examples of a hybrid flood control and ecological restoration project.

By using landscape solutions to reduce flooding, SWA Group also restored the ecological function of the bayou and gave Houstonians access to the waterway. The designers regraded the steep banks, removing nearly 31,000 cubic yards (23,700 cubic meters) of soil. This significantly increases storm water storage capacity and provides access to the park as well as views into the bayou from the surrounding buildings, streets, and freeways. The erosional banks of the bayou were stabilized with gabions filled with reused crushed concrete; 14,000 tons of concrete were salvaged from demolition projects and used to fill the metal mesh cages. Water can flow through the gabions, creating a complex edge between water and land that disperses the energy of both storm water and the waterway, helping to reduce erosion throughout the bayou.

Invasive plants were removed, and native and naturalized plants that can withstand flooding were selected for the riparian edge. In floods, the extensive planted edge helps to filter trash and sediment from the water, and like the gabion edges, the plantings disperse some of the energy of the water, helping to limit erosion. The designers selected plants that could stabilize the banks with deep roots and lateral rhizomes, such as Mexican petunia. And throughout, planting was designed to create a beautiful park and to assist in wayfinding. Ferns, Mexican petunia, and Louisiana iris add beauty to the park, and perennial plantings at the access points form gateways into the park and help to orient visitors.

Connecting Houston to its bayou is one of the signal achievements of the project. The 1.4 miles (2.3 kilometers) of trails within the promenade connect to 20 miles (32 kilometers) of trails throughout the bayou and link downtown Houston to the larger urban context. Twelve new entrances connect the downtown street grid to the promenade with ramps that provide access for bikes and strollers. Several of the trails end at the water with boat launches, making canoeing and kayaking the bayou possible. Four of the entrances are marked by new art pieces, and all have iconic decorative planting, forming enticing gateways to the bayou. Signage helps visitors find their way and also educates them about the bayou ecosystem.

And "moon phase" lighting subtly connects visitors to natural cycles while also providing a sense of safety in the park. Lights on the underside and columns of the freeway slowly change color over the month, brightening to white at the full moon and fading to indigo at the new moon. Having darker lights during the darker skies minimizes light pollution, which can severely impact nocturnal insects and migratory birds. The lighting, along with open views into and out of the park,

"Moon phase" lighting slowly changes color with the changing phases of the moon, subtly connecting visitors to the rhythms of nature.

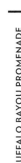

BUFFALO BAYOU PROMENADE

and open planting, has improved the sense of safety along the bayou. Along with an extensive program of events, this is bringing more people back to the water's edge, where they can reconnect with the plants and animals of the bayou and with its rhythms of flooding and calm.

By improving and revealing an existing ecosystem, Buffalo Bayou Promenade gives Houstonians extraordinary connections to an urban wild: a bayou that floods and recedes, the migratory patterns of indifferent animals, the horror of predator and prey, and the beauty of songbirds.

**Brackish stream restoration and park, incorporating playgrounds, recreation paths, and sports fields**

———

**VELSEN-NOORD, THE NETHERLANDS**

**DESIGNED BY**
Bureau B+B urbanism and landscape architecture in collaboration with Atelier de Lyon (both of Amsterdam)

**COMPLETED IN 2012**

**47 ACRES / 19 HECTARES**

The park has a stream-lined aesthetic: the concrete sweeps in long curves, and steel bridges have a thin profile.

Sweeping lines of concrete channels carry the reclaimed Scheybeeck through the park.

The channel ends in a new depression in the land, where salt water from the North Sea Canal mixes with the freshwater Scheybeeck to form a brackish marsh.

Newly created marshes fill an ecological need in the region, where such brackish marshes used to be a prolific habitat.

———

# WIJKEROOGPARK

When a stream is contained within two thin, parallel concrete lines that seem to dash into the distance, curving gently or sharply between straight sections, widening and narrowing, there seems no other word for it but *streamlined*. The Scheybeeck in Wijkeroogpark is an elegant, streamlined watercourse that also performs a host of ecological functions in a region where the landscape has been highly engineered. The project restores in places, and newly creates in others, portions of a freshwater stream that was once imprisoned in a culvert, and it reclaims some of the brackish marsh habitat that was lost to provide land for necessary housing.

In the early 2000s, the municipalities of Heemskerk, Beverwijk, and Velsen-Noord in western Holland collaborated to design a district plan to connect, protect, and restore landscape systems. The Green and Water Plan of 2009 connects the cities to their dunes, rivers, and polders by linking a set of parks with Green Routes through the region, and expanding existing parks or creating new parks to form a continuous landscape infrastructure. One route, centered on the Scheybeeck stream, highlights lost dune streams and restores some of the brackish ecotypes that historically occupied this landscape.

Historically, the Scheybeeck was a headwater of a hydrologic system that began in the inner dunes of the North Sea, flowed south to a brackish inland lake called Wijkermeer, and joined the tidal IJ River, which flowed east past Amsterdam into the Zuiderzee, a large inland bay off the North Sea. Although the Scheybeeck begins about 3 miles (5 kilometers) east of the North Sea, the watercourse traveled a counterclockwise spiraling route of approximately 93 miles (150 kilometers) to enter the sea far up the coast.

The hydrology of the Netherlands has, of course, been engineered for centuries, but a land-reclamation campaign in the mid-nineteenth and early twentieth centuries radically altered the Scheybeeck's hydrologic and ecologic setting. In 1876, the North Sea Canal opened, connecting Amsterdam directly to the sea. The Scheybeeck, portions of which had been buried in underground pipes in the previous decade, now flowed the direct 3 miles (5 kilometers) to the sea, with none of the complex brackish lakes, rivers, and marshes between. In 1932, construction was completed on a dike containing the Zuiderzee, which then became a freshwater lake (renamed the IJsselmeer and later divided to include a second lake, the Markermeer). Through a system of polders (drained areas of marsh or shallow lake enclosed by dikes), large swaths of land were reclaimed for residential development and farming. In the process, the complex gradient from freshwater to salt water was significantly reduced in the region.

The Scheybeeck was one of many dune streams feeding into the lake; now only traces of this system remain. Wijkeroogpark sits on what was formerly the bank of Lake Wijkermeer. The stream flowed into the lake at the north end of the park, where traces of an oxbow remain. As part of the larger Green and Water Plan, Bureau B+B was charged with restoring a portion of the stream as a centerpiece of the park, but also restoring brackish habitat that once occupied swaths of this landscape.

Wijkeroogpark restores some of the ecological complexity of the Scheybeeck and provides opportunities for people to interact with it. Some of the new 0.9-mile (1.5-kilometer) watercourse follows the old stream; other portions are newly

By varying the use of five concrete profiles, the designers created a variety of conditions, from narrow, constrained channel to wide marsh.

The park is designed for a wide variety of active and passive recreation within a program of ecological restoration.

Flowing south and pooling in a new brackish marsh before entering the sea canal, the stream stitches through the center of the park.

ECOLOGICAL URBANISM

16

Two concrete elements
set close together
create a thin, rapid
section of the stream.

constructed as part of the larger open space plan. The designers were not trying to recreate a historic stream. Rather, they were recovering ecological structures and functions within a radically altered cultural setting.

The stream's natural level is 12 inches (30 centimeters) above ground level, and a full 39 inches (100 centimeters) above the drainage ditches in the surrounding polder, which gave the designers unusual opportunities to design complex inter-actions with the stream. To prevent the park from becoming soggy and to enable the stream to reach the sea dike, the designers needed to bound the stream in some way. To guide the stream through the park, they created precast concrete elements in five different profiles. A wide variety of stream conditions is created by varying which profiles are used, whether one edge is hardened or two, and how far apart the two concrete elements are. At some times, the stream feels as if it were still in its former channel, bursting through the surface of the earth. At other times, it is linear, dynamic, and futuristic. And in other moments, the stream has a softer aesthetic, overflowing a grassed edge and pooling against the enclosing berms.

Because the stream regularly overflows into the newly graded park, the areas with a single concrete edge direct surplus water into temporary marshes, while in other areas the surrounding topography is depressed to create ponds and pools. At the southern terminus, where the park meets the sea dike, the ground is depressed into a large basin, and the concrete edges end dramatically. Freshwater from the Scheybeeck flows into the basin, and brackish water from the North Sea Canal is allowed in as well, mixing to create a brackish marsh. Wetland plants grow up against the aerodynamic curves of the concrete stream, providing a stark contrast of forms. Throughout the park, the pools and marshes, meadows and scrub recreate formerly prolific habitat for plants and animals.

The park has a clean, streamlined aesthetic. Walking and biking paths intertwine with the stream, which appears and disappears as visitors move through the park. Where the paths cross the stream, thin steel bridges seem to hover over the concrete edges. Along the route, the stream widens into a water garden, with paving and seating around it, on the same axis with two blocks of residential open space outside the park. The water garden creates an elegant terminus to the neighborhood axis and draws the neighborhood into the life of the stream. Farther south, the stream opens up again; the concrete forms draw apart into a wide, shallow pool with a crenellated plan, forming a children's play pool. Boulders in the stream encourage children to form and reform the stream, fostering playful manipulation of water. At the southern end, a fishpond can also be used for skating in the winter.

Throughout the park, the designers carefully filled in sheltering wooded areas and framing allees, and selected trees for removal to accommodate marshes and landscape rooms. The tree and shrub planting encloses the various ponds along the stream and frames long views through the park to the various water bodies. These views draw the neighborhood in and highlight the newly recreated marshes and stream.

Wijkeroogpark restores ecological structure and function to a formerly culverted stream. The marshes it restores are vital habitat patches, albeit rather small stepping-stones toward the large lakes of the former Zuiderzee. The park's clean, contemporary forms highlight the idea that ecological restoration need not deny human history. The concrete elements perform a useful function in directing the water toward the brackish canal, but they also recall the industrial history of the stream, serving as a cautionary reminder of both the power and the oversights of technology. And the sweeping, elegant lines are a powerful place-making device, anchoring the park firmly in the city's imagination.

Landscape-based climate-change-resilience plan, providing flood control as well as stream restoration, playgrounds, recreation paths and fields, and a brackish marsh

———

**KOKKEDAL, DENMARK**

**DESIGNED BY**
Schønherr A/S (Aarhus, Denmark)
with Bjarke Ingels Group
(Copenhagen) and Rambøll Danmark
A/S (Copenhagen)

**DESIGN COMPLETED IN 2012**

**170 ACRES / 69 HECTARES**

# KOKKEDAL CLIMATE ADAPTATION PLAN

Throughout the town plan, flood storage basins necessary for large storms are designed to serve on dry days as lawns and meadows.

———

**195**

In 2007 and 2010, Kokkedal, a suburb approximately 20 miles north of Copenhagen, experienced severe flooding along the Usserød River. After decades of development, it was clear that the city's storm water sewer system was inadequate. Town planners decided to turn the problem of reengineering the storm sewer into an opportunity for a visionary demonstration project based not only on climate projections but also on economic and demographic projections.

The climate adaptation plan links the town center, at left, with the Usserød valley, at right, through a series of water channels, basins, and marshes. The confluence of the Donse and Usserød rivers is at the bottom of the plan.

Permanent water remains at all times, enlivening the city. This plan diagram shows the linear forms of recirculation water channels and fountains in the city core as well as the ever-present rivers.

Smaller floods fill the storage system of infiltration basins, swales, and marshes. This low-flood plan diagram shows water filling a series of swales, rain gardens, and ponds, slowing the flow of storm water into the river.

This section looking north shows that by allowing most flooding to occur in the east, the plan keeps the west side open for recreational activities.

The Kokkedal Climate Adaptation Plan is the largest Danish urban retrofit for climate change to date, but it goes far beyond an impact-resilient urban design. The plan begins with strategies to mitigate the negative impacts of climate change and turns them into urban amenities, improvements to the functioning of the local ecosystem, and sources of civic pride and local identity. The suburban retrofit, designed by a team led by Schønherr, posits that the technical is social and the social is technical, that engineered solutions to infrastructural problems should also be solutions to social and ecological problems. The proposed land-scape-based infrastructure is designed to slow water flow, allow groundwater recharge, and remove pollutants from the water. Recognizing that flood storage will be used very infrequently, the channels and storage areas are designed as connecting paths, recreation fields, and attractive social and education spaces for daily use in Kokkedal.

While climate prediction models vary widely, the conservative estimate for Kokkedal is that there will be more rain in the winter and less in the summer than currently. But those fewer summer rainstorms are predicted to be more intense than current ones, with a 20-to-40-percent increase in storm intensity. While the 2007 floods were caused by long, steady storms that left soils saturated, the 2010 floods were the result of brief, high-intensity storms and so gave a preview of how summer storms might impact the city in the future. In about an hour, the Usserød River rose more than 3 feet (0.9 meters), overwhelming the storm sewer system and flooding about fifty houses east of the river. The existing storm water system was not designed for such rapid, high-volume concentrations of water.

Planning for the future, the city determined the need for a resilient storm water infrastructure, adapted to this changed hydrologic context, that could absorb brief, intense storm volumes. The city held an invited competition, asking firms to design an urban landscape that solved the flooding problem and also addressed three additional challenges: integrate the rainwater system into the urban fabric in both wet and dry weather, use the hydrologic landscape to add cohesion and connectivity to the fragmented town, and provide open space for activities and chance meetings between residents. Schønherr provided an elegant three-level solution with permanent fountains, streams, and channels as well as broad green space throughout the city that is sculpted to provide flood storage and convey-ance in both moderate and extreme storms.

Kokkedal is situated immediately north of the confluence of the Usserød and Donse rivers, and the Usserød valley divides the eastern portions of the town. The valley, formed by glacial melting, has a constrained profile that leaves little room for a broad floodplain that could hold floodwater. And the region is increasingly being developed, with impervious surfaces replacing forests and meadows that

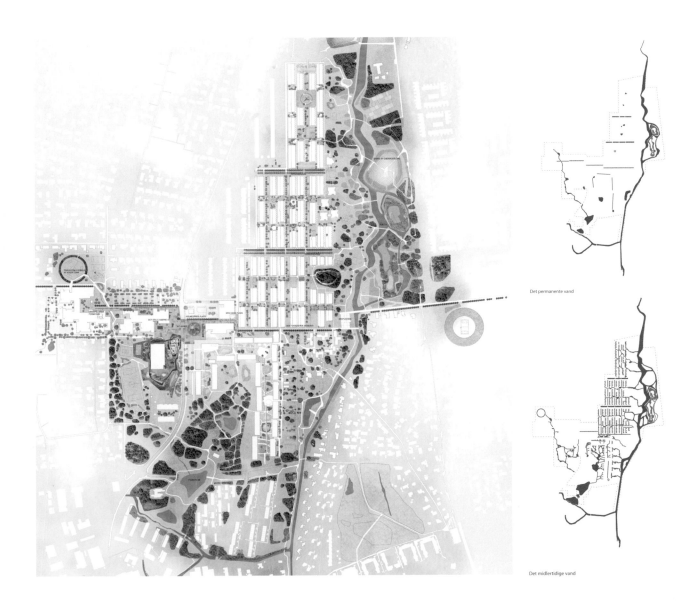

Det permanente vand

Det midlertidige vand

could absorb water and spread a storm's rainfall over time. As a result, the valley will continue to flood unless the rainfall is delayed upstream from reaching the river. The urban design is part of three active projects in Kokkedal: an open space plan to increase recreation opportunities in the district and connect urban centers like schools, a sport center, shopping districts, and a care center; a flood mitigation project for the Usserød River constructing a protecting dike and a double stream channel; and major renovations of the adjacent public housing.

Schønherr's proposal uses the river as the core of each of these plans and reframes the river as a community amenity and source of identity rather than a hazard. The plan uses three strategies to create a flood-resilient landscape that is a catalyst for urban and ecological improvements. It considers the storm water management landscape as open space first and flood-control basin second on the few days it is needed. It designs that open space based on the highest potential for ecological form, composition, and function. And it fully integrates that open space into the urban fabric, unifying the city, which has many north-south barriers such as rail-roads and highways, through the river valley.

The plan's primary goal is to increase urban resilience in the face of the predicted increase in flooding. Given the constraints on the rivers, the best way to do that is to minimize the rainwater reaching the river, to slow down the entire storm water chain. Allowing water to infiltrate to groundwater provides a slower, steadier flow to the river than the flash inputs from drainage pipes emptying directly into the river. The plan proposes disconnecting all storm water collectors—roofs, roads, sidewalks, and parking lots—from the piped sewer system and infiltrating all storm water locally in fields within the various neighborhoods and districts.

The water moves in a series of choreographed zones, from linear urban channels that convey water from the impermeable surfaces of the city, to vegetated open spaces that hold water and allow it to infiltrate into the ground, and thence to the river valley. In the urban zones, water takes architectural forms in channels, regular pools, and circular overflows. In the intermediate storage landscape, the water takes more irregular forms in deltas, ditches, and depressions, signifying a transition zone between the urban center and the river.

The project has three water systems: a permanent, recirculating water infrastructure; a storage system for five-year storms; and an overflow system for severe, twenty-year storms. The permanent system uses filtered rainwater for civic purposes. It creates visual connections between neighborhoods and to the river, and provides places for residents to interact and play with water on a regular basis. In the second layer of infrastructure, water is delayed in temporary holding areas, which are normally available as recreation space, or in alder swamps at the

In urban areas of the suburb, infiltration swales alongside roads slow and filter water, and allow it to infiltrate into groundwater.

Swales form the backbone of new social spaces, providing opportunities for planned or chance meetings with neighbors.

KOKKEDAL ADAPTATION PLAN

The redesigned Usserød valley adds back in ecotypes that have been destroyed over time, restoring the valley's previously rich biodiversity.

northern edge of Kokkedal. Lushly planted east-west paths convey water to the river, slowing it through rain gardens and ponds that filter pollutants and debris from the water before it enters the river. The system has a more linear form in the northern, more urban neighborhoods, and a more sinuous form in the southern, more suburban neighborhoods.

The climate adaptation plan elegantly weaves natural systems and processes into the urban fabric. By conceiving of the infrastructure as open space first, the plan ensures that a large portion of the city will be maintained as vegetation, with the possibility of habitat preservation and enhancement. Careful removal of some plantings and enhancement of others will allow social gathering places such as meeting spaces, swimming areas, and sports fields to be inserted into a rich land-scape palette of meadow and pasture, river and marsh, thicket and woodland. The Usserød valley was previously a species-rich area; the improved floodway will also

provide improved habitat for songbirds, bees and butterflies, amphibians and reptiles, and small mammals.

The portions of Kokkedal included in the competition contain a mix of glacial soils: meltwater clay, sand and gravel deposits, and postglacial peat. Each supports a different plant and animal association, and the designers carefully studied the ecological capacity of the valley. The open space is designed to improve the structure and function of the local ecosystem, with a transect of the ecotypes supported in this glacial meltwater valley. Existing, managed forests house mammals and raptors, while the shrubs and fruiting trees added to scrub and low forest provide nesting and feeding sites for songbirds. The plan recreates the former conditions of streams and wetlands: wooded wetlands provide cool, shady, wet areas suited to amphibians and reptiles; marshes provide habitat for insects that in turn are fed on by bats and barn swallows. And the enlarged and enhanced lakes

and deep marshes are home to amphibians, fish, and waterfowl such as geese, swans, ducks, and teal.

The catalyst for this blue-green infrastructure is the need to create places to slow, clean, and cool rainwater, and to give it an opportunity to infiltrate into the groundwater table rather than flow into the river. But by designing the space for the majority of dry days, the plan also creates opportunities for chance encounters between residents, enhancing the social cohesion of the town. The plan leverages the storm water system as an active recreation center and uses climate adaptation to foster urban vitality.

Kokkedal has connectivity problems. The town has many north-south barriers that prevent easy movement from east to west. Railroad tracks, highways, and the river obstruct easy communication between neighborhoods, leading to social fragmentation between different socioeconomic groups who live in different districts. Exacerbating this, the existing pedestrian paths are seen as unsafe; they are narrow and poorly lit, leading to very little pedestrian activity after dark.

The designers conceived of the river valley as a grand landscape room that opens up to and merges with the city fabric. The plan divides the valley into a river delta in the east and social (albeit floodable) spaces in the west. Lower slopes in the east accommodate flooding from smaller storms, while the western open space network provides higher ground that contains floodwaters in more severe storms. Knowing that people attract people, the designers have filled the western valley with activities, and a transverse trail links the town center to the newly activated glacial valley. Sports fields and recreation paths provide active destinations, and the slight hollows of the fields fill in low-intensity storms and overflow to the river

Play areas for children allow them to explore the river ecology.

202

ECOLOGICAL URBANISM

in extreme storms. Community gardening plots and gathering places are quiet areas for meeting new or old friends. A large paved area can be used as plaza or amphitheater and also provides an accessible route to the valley's trails. A water play area allows wading and swimming without endangering habitat areas. And throughout, the plan proposes clearing vegetation for habitat enhancement but also to allow long views in and out, improving the sense of safety. Water is designed as a thread binding the community, a meeting site, a place for joyful play, festive events, and education. New bridges and trails, and a new path network the river valley.

In the town center, the plan proposes three novel urban elements that collect rainwater, people, and activity, called by the designers a tapestry, a lawn, and an island. The tapestry is the urban blue fabric, a connective, paved network. At the center of the plan, a round plaza fills with storm water and recirculates the water in a play pool. Canals collect rainwater and direct it to storage hollows in the valley but also recirculate the water in blue threads that stitch the nodes of the town center together and to the valley; the learning canal outside the Kokkedal School contains play equipment such as an Archimedes screw, a piston pump, dams, locks, and wave pools, allowing children to explore the element that threads through the town. The lawn, at the southern edge of the town center, contains and connects significant sports facilities, a sports hall, a track, and playing fields along a meandering stream that drains south to the Donse River. Here too, sports fields are a primary defense against floods; the fields hold rainwater in heavy storms, alleviating the influx into the rivers. The third urban element, the island, provides an anchor and a link for the city center and the valley. Here, a hill crowned with a water tower reinforces the water-based identity of Kokkedal, and space is provided for social activities requested by residents: the existing sports hall for changing and for locking belongings; hills for biking and skating; and, in a district where few people have private garages or driveways, a shared area for working on cars and car washing.

The Kokkedal Climate Adaptation Plan is a forward-looking urban design that engages the uncertainty of the future in a hopeful and beautiful design. While climate models predict a wide range of future scenarios, all indications point to a significantly altered climate context in the future. Cities are long-term proposals, and our cities will need to respond with the long future in sight. If recent events are indicators, it is often the poorest, most vulnerable members of society who suffer the most in "natural" disasters. In Kokkedal, many of the neighborhoods immediately adjacent to the Usserød valley are public housing. The adaptation plan turns urban vulnerability into a flood solution that fosters social capital and ecological health.

# EDIBLE LANDSCAPES
## Agriculture in the City

Public Farm 1 in
Queens, New York.

**THE EARLIEST CITIES** included space for their provisioning within the city walls. Countless examples exist, but the Nolli map of Rome from 1748 is a well-known illustration, showing gardens, orchards, vineyards, and croplands within the city walls. With industrialization, food production was often displaced outside the city center (and, obviously, even in preindustrial cities, the hinterland was vital to the life of the city, for produce and crops as well as meat and dairy). Factors in this displacement included rising land values; efficiencies of scale for food production, processing, and distribution; and concern over the cleanliness of the urban environment.

Since the 1860s, urban food production has waxed and waned in popularity, usually in direct relation to the economy. Recessions, depressions, and wars have all led to resurgences in urban agriculture, whether in the potato patches of the 1890s, the Depression gardens of the 1930s, the victory gardens of World Wars I and II, or the more recent urban homesteading movement. Typically, these movements, however popular and successful, have not lasted once the external social or economic stress was removed. Urban gardens and farms are attractive solutions on underused and low-value lands; they are less attractive (to land owners and developers) when land values and development pressures increase. And industrial food systems are undeniably convenient. Raising and processing food is time consuming and often difficult.

And yet, urban farming persists and is experiencing a surge of interest. A 2012 survey by the American Community Gardening Association noted a 34 percent increase in the number of community gardens in the previous five years. The survey noted that the most common urban farming was in community gardens, with public housing and school gardens a distant second and third. While some of the recent interest must surely be attributed to the economic recession beginning in 2007, some is not based on economics. Deep mistrust of the industrial food system exists. The continued streamlining of the food supply system means that more food passes through fewer processing and distribution sites, making the food supply highly vulnerable. Furors over mad cow disease in the late 1990s and "pink slime" in 2012 have made the quality of our meat supply suspect. From an ethical standpoint, the treatment of animals on industrial farms, the decreased biodiversity of ever-dwindling species of produce, and the unknown impact of genetically modified food crops on the surrounding ecosystem give consumers pause. The impacts on the earth of industrial farming—from the impact of fertilizers and farm waste on watersheds to the climatic impact of global food distribution systems with their heavy use of fossil fuels—concern many. Concerns about obesity and diabetes epidemics are giving rise to calls for more produce in the American diet. And from consumers comes increasing demand for food that is picked ripe and sold rapidly, for more variety and more flavor in their produce. Health, energy, economics—all are interwoven in the seemingly simple question "What's for dinner?"

All these issues—environmental, ecological, ethical, pragmatic, and sensual—are contributing to a resurgence in the design professions of studying and designing food systems that operate at smaller scales and in more integrated ways. Since 2000, the scholarship on food has proliferated: community gardens, food systems, agricultural urbanism, urban agriculture, local food, the 100-mile diet, slow food. While large-scale systems of production, processing, and distribution of our food are unlikely to disappear, designers are seeking ways to increase our food options and provide some portion of the urban food supply from within the city itself.

Landscape architects rarely design the sites of urban agriculture. These farms and gardens need designs, such as they are, that are flexible and respond to the needs of the farmers and gardeners, and to the crops themselves. Often the designs are quite simple, based on modular plots or rows, organized around the limits of an irrigation system, the size of equipment, or the reach of an arm. Like ecology, urban agriculture for the landscape architect is more of a conceptual than a physical site. Rather than designing places, landscape architects can help design systems, identifying connections between people, places, and the functions of growing, processing, selling, and consuming food and reusing waste within the city. By considering urban agriculture, designers can include that as part of the program for a park, a residential development, or a community center.

The American Planning Association describes urban farming as commercial, noncommercial, or a hybrid and further distinguishes between the purposes of urban agriculture. Farms or gardens may be growing produce primarily for consumption, sale or donation, education, or economic or community development. The projects in this chapter show that range of activity, as well as the variety of sites available for food production in a city: building walls, roofs, and facades; abandoned or underused lots; brownfield sites. The projects show relatively permanent solutions—in-ground and structured—as well as modular and transient systems that address the land tenure concerns of urban farms.

A rooftop garden shows the potential for and challenges of farming above ground level. In Chicago, the Gary Comer Youth Center Roof Garden is a noncommercial edible garden with a social and educational mission. The center provides a quiet, safe refuge from an economically and socially troubled neighborhood, and gives children a tangible way to impact their environment. Studies have shown that this ability to change even a small physical space can ameliorate feelings of helplessness in the face of large-scale systems (social, economic) over which individuals feel they have no control. Gardening empowers gardeners.

A community garden in Seattle proposes gardening as a public and social activity. The Beacon Food Forest is designed using the permaculture principle of mixed horizontal layers, from roots and ground covers to canopy trees and vines in a single garden bed. It is also intended to be completely public—anyone can harvest the produce—to share the harvest with neighbors who need food and to encourage neighbors to engage with the garden and each other. Gardens grow communities as well as produce.

Two modular farms address the difficulty of land tenure in cities as well as concerns about contaminated soils in urban sites. In Berlin, Prinzessinnengarten is an example of guerilla gardening: farmers are occupying contaminated land with a modular container farm. This is grassroots gardening with a social mission; all the plots are open to all, the produce is available to anyone, and there are events and a café that encourage social activity on what was an abandoned lot in the shadow of the Berlin Wall. In New York, at the Museum of Modern Art's P.S.1 Contemporary Art Center, P.F.1 (Public Farm 1) displayed a similar modular approach, although with a more top-down design, and was intended as a demonstration of the potential of modular urban gardening. By raising some of the gardening modules on a structure, the designers created an undulating topography with landscapes above and below the thin skin of agriculture.

Finally, the Grünewald Public Orchard illustrates the integration of food production into the urban fabric, showing that food production can serve more than one purpose in a city. Paths and plazas are organized with plants that also produce food: fruit trees and berry bushes. Their color and structure help orient residents and visitors; espaliered trees line major paths, and courtyards are organized by food production (fruit, nut, berry) and color of flowers, fruit, and fall foliage. Often, agriculture is considered as a thing in and of itself (a farm, a greenhouse, a community garden). The Grünewald Public Orchard reminds designers that agricultural production can be an additional benefit of a vibrant neighborhood design.

**Rooftop garden to teach students the skills of growing, processing, preserving, and cooking food**

---

**CHICAGO, ILLINOIS**

**DESIGNED BY**
Peter Lindsay Schaudt, Hoerr Schaudt
Landscape Architects (Chicago)

John Ronan Architects (Chicago),
building design

**COMPLETED IN 2006**

**8,160 SQUARE FEET /
760 SQUARE METERS**

# GARY COMER YOUTH CENTER ROOF GARDEN

Two stories above the street on Chicago's South Side, children learn to garden at the Gary Comer Youth Center. In a neighborhood with little access to either healthy food or safe outdoor spaces, the center's rooftop haven turns a working vegetable garden into a place of beauty and respite. The garden grows not only organic vegetables but also the students' skills in horticulture, nutrition, small business management, and more. And it serves as a model for urban agriculture.

The rooftop garden at the Gary Comer Youth Center is a safe place for children to play and learn.

Children learn horticulture and nutrition in the garden, and the produce is served in the café downstairs. But the lessons of the garden are not limited to classes about food; business, math, and environmental science classes are also held here.

---

The Gary Comer Youth Center is housed in a brightly patterned three-story, 75,000-square-foot (7,000-square-meter) building centered on a double-height gymnasium. Above the gymnasium is the roof garden; a taller outer ring containing offices, computer lab, library, and meeting rooms surrounds that central block. As a result, the roof garden is completely enclosed by the third floor; students moving through the hallways on that floor have continuous views out to the garden. The lines of the window mullions extend to the horizontal surface of the garden through pathways that divide the garden into a series of linear planting beds. Circular skylights provide daylight to the gymnasium below and create a playful pattern in the garden, and the thick and thin bands of soil are planted with decorative flowers, shade-giving grasses, and produce.

The center is located in Chicago's South Side neighborhood of Grand Crossing. The neighborhood is a triangle bounded by I-90 to the west, railroad tracks to the east, and Oakwoods Cemetery to the north. Close-set one- and two-story homes predominate in the neighborhood, with Hoard Park and Paul Revere Elementary School at its center. Benefactor Gary Comer, founder of the clothing company Land's End, grew up in the neighborhood. His original plan for the building was to provide a practice space for the South Shore Drill Team, a performance group founded to give students a positive activity and discipline that would help them stay in school. Initial requests were simple: heated space, few windows to discourage drive-by shootings, easily maintained surfaces for the inevitable graffiti. With Comer's growing enthusiasm for the project, what the neighborhood eventually got was a building that met those pragmatic requirements and then kept going. The center provides safe, engaging places for students to learn computer skills, do their homework and receive tutoring, play basketball, dance, record music, create art, and—on the green roof—learn to garden, cook, and manage a small business.

The neighborhood is a food desert; a local gas station is the only place to purchase food in the community. As is the case in many food deserts, the lack of food options makes it difficult for residents to buy fresh, healthy produce. The rooftop garden teaches students how to grow produce, and in a first-floor kitchen, they also learn how to prepare and preserve the harvest. Students who work in the garden are also able to take produce home to their families. The garden annually produces more than 1,000 pounds of organic vegetables, which are used in the first-floor café, sold to local restaurants and at a farmer's market, and eaten by the students themselves.

While growing produce is important, the garden was conceived as a place for students to learn and to prepare for college or jobs. In addition to the horticulture and nutrition curriculum, the garden is used in math, business, environmental science, and green roof technology courses. Students in a Green Career Exploration

program learn about organic gardening and small business management, and in the summer earn a stipend for their work. And children from Revere Elementary School come to the center for gardening classes on the roof.

Soil vitality is a concern on the roof. The growth medium is a deep 18 to 24 inches (45 to 60 centimeters) to allow healthy root growth. (In comparison, the thinnest sedum green roofs have as little as 2 inches, or 5 centimeters, of medium, and 4 to 6 inches, 10 to 15 centimeters, is considered adequate for most living roofs.) With depth comes weight, especially when the soil is saturated. The lightweight medium is blended of lightweight aggregate for easy drainage, sphagnum moss for water retention, compost for plant health, and organic fertilizer. The soil is regularly fed with compost tea, and crops are rotated to add nutrients and prevent soil depletion. But the designers acknowledge that the soil's longevity is unknown.

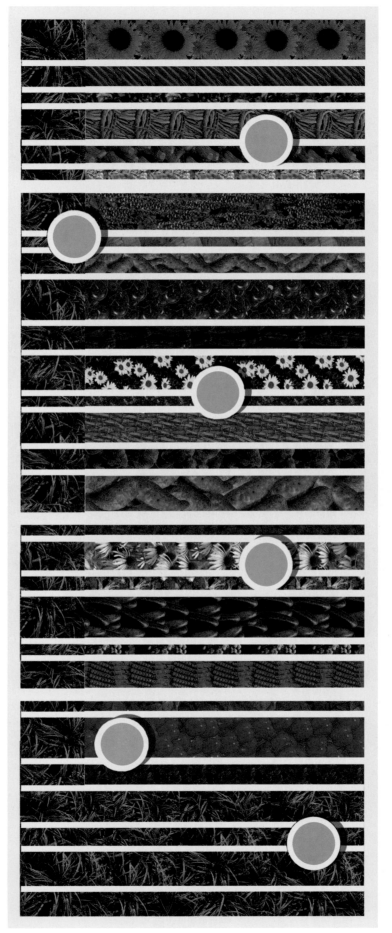

Sunflower Mixture
with Tulip Bulbs

Carrots

Purple Leaf Lettuce

Beans

Hot Peppters

Oregano / Basil

Foxglove Mixture
with Daffodil Bulbs

Cabbage

Sweet Potato

Tomato

Zucchini

Daisy / Aster Mixture
with Tulip Bulbs

Rosemary / Dill

Okra

Romaine Lettuce

Potato

Parsley

Coneflower / Beard Tongue Mixture
with Muscari Bulbs

Broccoli

Cucumber

Chives

Peas

Butterhead Lettuce

Yellow Bell Pepper

Lily Mixture
with Tulip Bulbs

Creeping Lilyturf

The garden is planted in a mix of crops, herbs, grasses, and flowers, and crops are rotated to maintain healthy soil.

———

Skylights enliven the garden and bring light into the gym below.

**214**

EDIBLE LANDSCAPES

To grow good produce, farms must grow good soil. At the Comer Center, the garden is being monitored to see how soils change over time and to generate best practices for future rooftop gardening projects.

The garden has an innovative microclimate design, manipulating wind and shade and reusing heat from the building to expand the seasonal comfort and the growing season. Tall grasses are located to provide shade in summer, and sun and wind studies were used to best arrange the surrounding walls to buffer from wind in the winter and provide shade in summer. Evapotranspirative cooling helps moderate summer heat, and warm air from a large circular exhaust vent helps to keep the

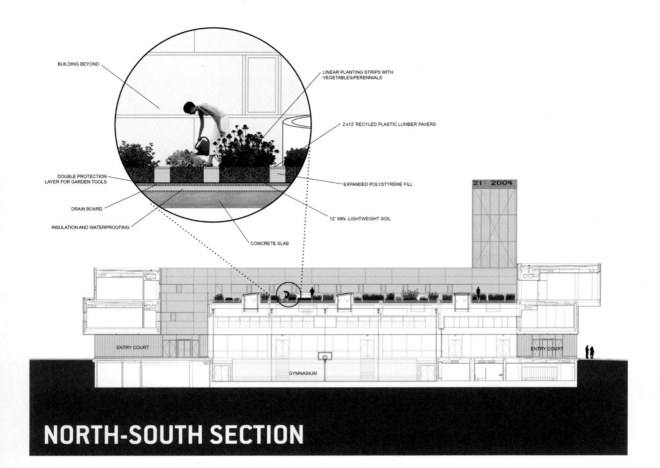

BUILDING BEYOND

LINEAR PLANTING STRIPS WITH VEGETABLES/PERENNIALS

2'x12' RECYLED PLASTIC LUMBER PAVERS

DOUBLE PROTECTION LAYER FOR GARDEN TOOLS

EXPANDED POLYSTYRENE FILL

DRAIN BOARD

12" MIN. LIGHTWEIGHT SOIL

INSULATION AND WATERPROOFING

CONCRETE SLAB

21 : 2004

ENTRY COURT

ENTRY COURT

GYMNASIUM

# NORTH-SOUTH SECTION

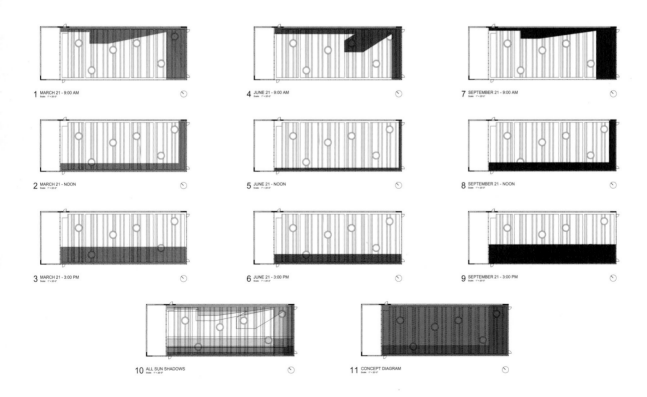

1 MARCH 21 - 9:00 AM
Scale: 1" = 20'-0"

4 JUNE 21 - 9:00 AM
Scale: 1" = 20'-0"

7 SEPTEMBER 21 - 9:00 AM
Scale: 1" = 20'-0"

2 MARCH 21 - NOON
Scale: 1" = 20'-0"

5 JUNE 21 - NOON
Scale: 1" = 20'-0"

8 SEPTEMBER 21 - NOON
Scale: 1" = 20'-0"

3 MARCH 21 - 3:00 PM
Scale: 1" = 20'-0"

6 JUNE 21 - 3:00 PM
Scale: 1" = 20'-0"

9 SEPTEMBER 21 - 3:00 PM
Scale: 1" = 20'-0"

10 ALL SUN SHADOWS
Scale: 1" = 20'-0"

11 CONCEPT DIAGRAM
Scale: 1" = 20'-0"

garden warmer in the winter. The garden microclimate is up to 20 degrees warmer in winter and 10 degrees cooler in summer than the surrounding neighborhood. The addition of crop hoops further extends the growing season, allowing cold-hardy produce planting throughout Chicago's famously cold and snowy winter.

The Comer Center rooftop garden focuses on education and skill building. While learning to grow produce, students also learn nutrition, cooking, and healthy habits, as well as business management skills. The program has been so successful that it has expanded to a 15,000-square-foot (1,400-square-meter) community garden across the street. The garden is on a brownfield—a former gas station and petrochemical distribution center. The land was cleaned to the EPA's most stringent residential standard and now hosts an organic farm that can grow fruit and nut trees as well as the types of row crops that grow in the rooftop garden. Like the rooftop garden, education is key at the community garden. Both gardens provide structured programming to reconnect students with the processes of growing, processing, preserving, and cooking food. And in this neighborhood where being outside can be frightening and even dangerous, the rooftop garden provides a calm, secure place for students to be outside, engaged in hands-on learning.

The building buffers the garden from wind, creating a warm microclimate and extending the growing season.

The design team used shadow studies to determine the best building mass and to locate plants.

**Public food production in a neighborhood permaculture orchard and gardens**

———

**SEATTLE, WASHINGTON**

**DESIGNED BY**
Glenn Herlihy

Margarett Harrison, Harrison Design Landscape Architecture (Seattle)

Jenny Pell, Permaculture Now! (Seattle)

**PHASE 1 COMPLETED IN 2013**

**7 ACRES / 2.8 HECTARES**

# BEACON FOOD FOREST

Building community while building a garden: volunteers have built sheds and terraced the sloped site at this new public garden

———

**219**

Two miles south of downtown Seattle in the Beacon Hill neighborhood, a narrow, sloping plot adjacent to a public park is being transformed into an edible arboretum, with the food grown available to anyone who wants to pick it. The Beacon Food Forest will be one of the largest food forests on public land in the United States, designed according to permaculture principles. One board member describes it as a place to gather community, grow food, rehabilitate the ecosystem, revitalize public land, improve public health, create awareness of the impact of food production on climate change, and increase the safety of the local food supply.

The Beacon Food Forest develops overlooked land as urban agriculture, with two significant differences from the usual community garden model. First, the land is being developed as a food forest, a permaculture design strategy of multilayered planting. Second, the food forest is intended to be a community resource—the food grown will be available to anyone who wants to harvest it. The food forest began in 2009 as a class project in a permaculture course. Glenn Herlihy, a member of the neighborhood group Jefferson Park Alliance (JPA), spearheaded the project as a way to think more creatively about the use of public land in cities. In 2000, Seattle had passed the Pro-Parks Levy, a property tax of $0.35 per $1000 property value, to fund the creation of new parks and the stewardship and improvement of existing parks throughout the city. Jefferson Park, in Beacon Hill, had been allocated $8 million from the levy for development. The 43-acre

(17-hectare) site had held two Seattle Public Utility open reservoirs, one of which was decommissioned and one of which was redesigned as a buried reservoir. The resulting land was redeveloped as an open lawn, playing fields, an amphitheater, a playground, and a skate park. To the west of the new park, a 7-acre (2.8-hectare) sliver of sloping land remained outside of the park plan. Herlihy and his project team proposed turning this slope into a productive community asset—the food forest.

The JPA supported the idea, and a steering committee, which later became the Friends of Beacon Food Forest, was formed to pursue it. The city of Seattle awarded the project a $20,000 grant to design the food forest in greater detail, including public input from neighborhood meetings, and subsequently provided $100,000 for construction of the first phase, and $86,000 for the design and construction of a community building and tool shed. Beacon Hill is one of the most diverse zip codes in the United States, and the food forest has garnered immense community support through vigorous outreach. Residents of the neighborhood are from a wide range of backgrounds. Japanese, Chinese, Vietnamese, Laotian, Korean, Filipino, Samoan, Native American, Caucasian, and African American populations all call Beacon Hill home. At public meetings, community celebrations, and work parties, neighbors have been actively drawn into the project. As a result, the plant palette has grown from about a hundred plants to more than a thousand, including edible plants from neighbors' homelands around the globe.

The primary idea of a food forest is to mimic the self-regulating systems found in nature. They contain up to seven layers of plants: a canopy of larger trees; an

The project began to take physical form at the "groundmaking," with community members breaking sod and mulching with cardboard sheets, compost, and wood chips.

———

From the beginning, the project has included design feedback and construction contributions from the entire community. Here, community members cut cardboard boxes to flat sheets for mulch.

BEACON FOOD FOREST

understory of smaller, often dwarf varieties of trees; a shrub layer; an herbaceous layer of vegetables and perennials; root crops; ground covers; and climbers. Plants are clustered in "guilds"—communities of plants that benefit each other and provide habitat for beneficial animals and insects. Wide, flat flowers such as yarrow or parsley, for instance, provide habitat for ladybugs, which feed on harmful insects such as aphids. And flowering plants provide food for pollinators, which help ensure high crop yields. Monocultures and large swaths of individual plants are avoided so that outbreaks of pests are avoided, since there isn't an easy passage from one plant to the next. The plants are also selected to improve soil health: plants such as lupine add nitrogen to the soil, which is needed for fruit-bearing trees. And plants such as artichoke act as natural mulch, preventing weeds and adding nutrients to the soil. Obviously, plant, soil, and insect knowledge is needed for initial plant selection and location, and ongoing observation and adjustment is required, especially in the first few years, to establish a healthy food forest.

In early visioning exercises during park events, community members placed signs on the site where they envisioned various plants.

At the Beacon Food Forest, edible foods are clustered in several areas and guilds. A nut grove will provide almonds, hazelnuts, beechnuts, and walnuts, as well as understory shrubs, to feed both people and animals. An orchard will provide fruits: apples, pears, and plums, with blueberries and cane fruit such as raspberries planted beneath. A native guild will contain Seattle native plants for education, consumption, and habitat. There will be edible arboreta showcasing trees from around the globe and reflecting the multi-ethnic neighborhood of Beacon Hill. There will be P-Patches, as Seattle calls its community garden allotments, as well as tree patches: garden plots that include a fruit or nut tree. These more traditional community garden plots will be individually leased and gardened, and the produce grown in them will belong to the garden plot leaseholder. These plots will provide continuity and stability to the food forest experiment. Enclosed in this edible landscape will be open space for play and gathering, and a children's play area.

The most unusual aspect of the Beacon Food Forest is the idea that all the food grown will be publicly available for anyone who wants to harvest it. This is just one visible aspect of a deep community-based process. Permaculture seeks, among other things, to help plants help themselves: to select and organize plants that form mutually beneficial relationships. The Beacon Food Forest extends that idea to the human community. Urban agriculture and community gardens have been shown to have a dramatic impact on self-sufficiency. They provide food, but they also provide community, demonstrated to improve gardeners' emotional states; they provide health benefits from gardening; and they provide job skills, from

The Beacon Food Forest nestles on a steep slope, with terraces and guilds dividing the site into discrete areas.

223

BEACON FOOD FOREST

"soft skills" such as teamwork and social networking to technical and transferable skills. In Beacon Hill, the food forest has already provided cultural understanding between neighbors and a sense of empowerment as residents help create their own environment in a way that reflects themselves.

The community has built the garden in a series of work parties. Early visioning events got neighbors on-site and raised enthusiasm for the project, cultivating the community of gardeners as residents located flags to visualize the layout and filled in surveys about what activities they would like to see in the garden. Rather than a ground-breaking event, organizers hosted a ground-making day, with volunteers removing turf, adding compost to soils, and mulching with straw and cardboard. And the project has involved groups from outside the community. The sloping site is organized into terraces, which are structured with "urbanite" walls—retaining walls made from recycled concrete that the Seattle Department of Transportation had been stockpiling from demolition projects around the city. A University of Washington architecture class designed and built an interlocking set of pavilions to serve as a community living room, with covered benches and a toolshed framing a gathering space.

As the first phase of the Beacon Food Forest was being built in 2013, enormous community support already existed for the project, and many of its goals for community empowerment and engagement had already been achieved. What remains to be seen is the success of the forest itself. Will the system work as expected? Will the plants reach such a level of health and robustness that little maintenance is required? And will the free access to food result in overharvesting of the crops? Gardens require gardeners for success. Given the strong history of Seattle's P-Patch program, it is likely that the community gardens will thrive. With those, and with the community support already generated by the project, it seems likely there will be a committed group of gardeners at the Beacon Food Forest ensuring its productivity.

A community work party plants a guild of blueberries, sage, and sunflowers.

The garden pavilion, designed and built by University of Washington architecture students, provides storage, seating, and a community gathering area.

Nomadic community
garden, serving as a
center for strengthening
social ties and activism

———

**BERLIN, GERMANY**

**FOUNDED BY**
Marco Clausen and Robert Shaw

**COMPLETED IN 2009**

**21,500 SQUARE FEET /
2,000 SQUARE METERS**

# PRINZESSINNEN-GARTEN

The café, which serves
produce grown in the
garden, has proved a
popular neighborhood
center, serving as many
as two hundred meals
in an evening.

———

227

At the southeast edge of Moritzplatz, in Berlin, volunteers have
built a remarkable mobile garden on half an acre of land that has
remained undeveloped since the Second World War. The planting beds and structures are all demountable or transportable,
responding to an all-too-frequent concern for urban agriculture:
uncertainty of land lease. In response to this uncertainty, founders
Marco Clausen and Robert Shaw, along with more than 1,500
volunteers to date, have created a lush, vibrant community center
from found, recycled, and repurposed materials.

In this nomadic garden, tomatoes grow in milk cartons, onions in bright red plastic bakers' crates. They have put down perhaps-temporary roots in a long-neglected district. The garden site is the former home of a Wertheim department store that was heavily damaged by bombing in the Second World War and later demolished (aerial photos from 1953 show the building still standing, nearly surrounded by urban demolition). The site lay fallow for more than sixty years. It was two blocks south of the Berlin Wall, in West Berlin; Prinzenstrasse, the street forming the garden's western boundary, was one of the few crossings between the American Sector and the Russian Sector. Below ground, the Peter Behrens–designed subway station was the last stop in West Berlin before subway trains passed without

For years, the site lay fallow, used only intermittently as a car park, a market, or for ephemeral festivals.

Now, in addition to the productive gardens, the site includes a café and seating grove, a performance space, and a library, providing a social hub in the neighborhood.

USE OF SPACE
*in* prinzessinnengärten

**Materials**

Materials considered waste become re-used:
Workshops
Furniture cooperation
Re-use day
(recycling-upcycling)

**Garden Restaurant / Bar**

Cooking & Selling regional organic food and drinks.
Creates income for employees for farmers (CSA)
Financial support of non profit activities

**Urban Bees**

Collaborating with beekeeper in the City:
Pollinating plants in the garden
Beekeeping workshop
Honey

**Off-shoot Gardens**

Building gardens in kindergardens, schools, universities etc.
Building gardens in other cities (Hamburg, Colon, Baden Baden)
Creating a platform for consulting gardens ("common grounds")
Creating income for the gardeners

Mushrooms

Igaum Pale BLue Dot

**Stable + library**

Space for events, library, shelter from rain, workshops and meetings
Discussions, concerts and movies
Archive

Perennial Garden

**Bikes**

DIY Bike repair-workshop
Tools
Re-use day

Potatoe Project

Compost

Medicinal Plants

Dyeing Plants

**Kicker & Ping-Pong**

Playing
Relaxing
Chatting

**Raised Beds**

Exclusively communal raised beds (easily built out of plastic boxes, light and transportable)
Used to grow over 500 species of plants.
Production of vegetables for Restaurant and selling.

**Garden & Building container**

Tools
Furniture building
Learning to build
Seed storage
Offshoot gardens

**Info-box**

Guided Tours
Visitors can buy: compost
vegetables    rice sacks
plants    books
seeds    T-shirts etc...

Exhibition space
Workshops
Communication
Archive

Here visitors can get information about open days, plants and the garden

**Treibhaus**

**Ingredients:**

| | | | |
|---|---|---|---|
| Employees | Bees | Tools for: | 500 species of plants |
| Volunteers | Butterflies | Gardening | Seeds |
| Interns from schools & universities | Worms | Building | Wood (re-used) |
| (Voluntry Ecological Year) | Birds | Bicycles | Plastic boxes (re-used) |
| Local Community | Other micro-organisms | Upcycling | Rice sacks |
| Researchers | | | Containers (re-used) |
| Artists | | | Rice Sacks |
| Visitors | | | Pallets (re-used) |
| Collectives (using the space) | | | Soil and compost |
| School Groups | | | Other waste flows |
| | | | Unused City Space |
| | | | Water |

## USE OF SPACE
*in* prinzessinnen**gärten**

### Social

To sit, eat, relax, decelerate, meet, talk
For Events
For artists
For research
For projects

### Ecological

Habitat Improvement
Ecosystem Services
Sustainable Praxis
Biodiversity of crops.
Pollination

### Economic

Providing Income and Employment Opportunities
Neighbourhood regeneration
City tourist attraction
Market Space

### Political

Sustainable Food Systems
Re-imagine the City
Re-value green spaces
Active Citizenship
Campaigns

### Spaces for *Learning*

To grow food organically
About regional and seasonal food
Cooking and preserving food
Composting food waste
Available diversity of crops and seeds
To build furniture & planting solutions
To build and repair bicycles
To re-use materials

✳ Open project space

stopping through six East Berlin "ghost stations." For years, the site was a car park, temporary shops and markets, or unused.

Prinzessinnengarten (Princess Garden, named after the adjacent Prinzessinnenstrasse) is structured by two key strategies: creating community and mobile gardening. In 2009, Prinzessinnengarten founders Marco Clausen and Robert Shaw wanted to create an urban farm that would provide a model of mobility, occupation of derelict spaces, and the community-fostering power of gardens. They wanted to turn the underused site into a community garden to provide organic produce for the community but also to serve as a community hub where neighbors could work, learn about ecological farming and food preservation, and strengthen social ties in the process. Clausen and Shaw formed a nonprofit organization, Nomadisch Grün (Nomadic Green), and rented the lot on a short-term basis from the city.

From its first stages, the garden has been a volunteer and community effort. Shaw and Clausen ran a newspaper ad asking for help clearing the site, expecting

The garden provides a variety of social spaces, for education, relaxation, and play.

a dozen or so people to show up. Instead, more than 150 volunteers came and quickly cleared more than 2 tons of garbage from the site. While there is a regular core of about twenty volunteers, hundreds of people come to weekly open gardening hours, and by early 2013, more than a thousand volunteers had worked at the garden. Shaw and Clausen see the garden as a social space where "everybody can do their own thing; nobody has to do anything." Community members who work in the garden receive a 50-percent discount on produce, food from the on-site café, and plants. And because no minimum commitment is required, people can drop in, try out planting, weeding, or harvesting, and slowly grow commitment to the work and the place.

Over four years, the garden has expanded to include not only the vegetable plot but also the popular café (which sells up to two hundred dinners in an evening), a library of gardening references, a shop selling plants and herbs, meeting space, a children's playhouse, and beehives. This has been a community-based process; spaces have been added and altered as volunteers have suggested and implemented improvements. The central Berlin neighborhood of Kreuzburg, where the garden is located, has a large immigrant population; many members of the community come from rural backgrounds and have been able to provide gardening expertise and also bring seeds from their homes around Europe. Community gardeners currently grow more than five hundred plant varieties, including more than fifteen kinds of tomatoes, twenty varieties of potatoes, and seven types of carrots.

Prinzessinnengarten generates revenue through the sale of produce, prepared food and drinks at the café, and plants and herbs. It also generates some revenue through donations and crowdfunding. The income pays the lease for the site; when Nomadisch Grün initiated the garden, the city leased the land for one year, with an option to renew the lease annually.

Land tenure is often a problem for urban farming. Gardens are an attractive form of land banking; cities maintain ownership of land until it becomes valuable enough to develop at a profit, and the gardens help to create community and investor confidence in a neighborhood. Often, once gardens have had this effect, the gardens lose their leases, and the sites are developed. Recognizing that risk, Shaw and Clausen developed a modular garden around three ideas: maintaining the ability to move their investment, addressing the possibility of contaminated soils, and creating a prototype for the temporary occupation of unused land. Says Clausen, "It's a meanwhile-use project. Like a moving circus, we are kind of experts for temporary gardens. If the property is going to be sold, we'll move on to another place. Though we are willing to move, we still try to leave something behind, in the sense of empowerment."

Volunteers drop in to work in the garden as they are available. With no minimum work requirement, the garden allows volunteers to try different tasks, find activities they enjoy, and grow into gardeners.

The library contains references on gardening, composting, bee keeping, and other topics of interest to volunteers and visitors, and provides space for activities such as grant writing workshops.

PRINZESSINNENGARTEN

To address that uncertainty, the entire garden is mobile, constructed with industrial crates, milk cartons, rice bags, hollow masonry—any container that can be moved and can be repurposed to hold soil. The site is loosely structured; bark and gravel paths divide planting beds of weathered wooden crates, brightly colored plastic crates, large white sacks, and small blue cartons. In past years, volunteers have transported the entire garden by wheelbarrow to its winter home in the nearby markthalle (hall built to house weekly farmers markets). But while the garden can be physically moved, its highest value is in the social benefits it generates, which frequent moves would undermine. Workshops, meals, and daily work have made the garden a place where people want to spend time, socializing, working, people watching. Ironically, perhaps because of its novel mobile design, the garden has become so popular that many residents would like to see it become a protected, permanent institution.

In fall of 2012, the garden organizers learned that the city was negotiating with developers to sell the land. Despite the intentionally mobile nature of the garden, volunteers and visitors were dismayed and began a petition campaign that eventually garnered more than thirty thousand signatures. The petition to the city asked for a minimum five-year lease on the site, civic participation in the planning process, and integration of community gardens and similar community-based projects into the city's urban plans. In December 2012, the city agreed to transfer ownership of the property from the Berlin Property Fund (the city) to the Borough of Kreuzberg-Friedrichshain. The mayor of the borough has publicly expressed his support for Prinzessinnengarten, viewing it and similar projects as crucial to the success of the district. It appears that the mobile garden may be here to stay.

Bee-keeping workshops are popular. The bees help pollinate the produce and also make honey for use and sale.

————

Structures throughout the garden are made from reused and repurposed materials. A camping trailer has been outfitted as an information center, orienting visitors and volunteers.

The entire garden is designed to be moveable in the event that the land is sold to a developer.

Gardeners grow a wide range of produce. Many of the varieties are unusual, grown from seeds volunteers bring from their home countries.

Modular, elevated
installation treating urban
farming as sculpture

———

**QUEENS, NEW YORK**

**DESIGNED BY**
Amale Andraos and Dan Wood,
WORK Architecture Company
(New York City)

**STAGED IN 2008**

**11,000 SQUARE FEET /
1,000 SQUARE METERS**

# PUBLIC FARM 1

The farm rose up
and over a courtyard
wall, unifying two
distinct areas.

———

**235**

In the courtyard of the Museum of Modern Art's P.S.1 Contemporary Art Center, a folded plane of cardboard tubes and vegetation
seemed to hover in the air, touched down in the middle, and rose
to skim over a wall and into a second courtyard. Vegetation rose
above the plane and spilled down the edges, and where the form
touched down, it opened up to accommodate a pool and fountain. Dan Wood, one of the project's designers, wryly commented,
"It's probably one of the best folded cardboard farms in New York
City. At least in Queens."

WorkAC's P.F.1—Public Farm 1—seemed improbably light and simple. A modular skin of structural cardboard tubes, nearly 100 feet by 20 feet (30 meters by 6 meters), was raised 30 feet (9 meters) in the air at one end and 15 feet (4.5 meters) in the air at the other, supported by a forest of brightly painted cardboard tubes. Above was a quarter-acre (0.1-hectare) urban farm: each section of cardboard tube was planted with a different variety of produce, from beets and tomatoes to nasturtiums and herbs. The space created below was alternately a pavilion, a grotto, a playground. By elevating the vegetable garden, the designers made it into something much more.

Each summer, P.S.1 hosts a summer music festival, Warm Up!, that animates the museum courtyard in the evenings. And each year, MoMA / P.S.1 holds a competition, the Young Architect Program, to design a temporary installation to house and structure the summer festival. The program is simple: provide shade, seating, and water while dividing the two courtyards into outdoor rooms to provide performance and gathering spaces in a variety of sizes. Amale Andraos and Dan Wood, the principals at WorkAC, used the idea of the urban beach as a starting point for a project that frames the humble act of growing food as a social and urban revolution. They turned the rallying cry of the 1968 student protests in France, "Sous les pavés la plage" (beneath the cobblestones, the beach), into a new urban manifesto, "Sur les pavés la ferme" (above the street, the farm). The call to escape standardization for a life of individuality was reframed into a call for flexible modularity that allows the rediscovery of unique forms of productivity.

The project used modular construction and simple materials to create a farm that could be easily recreated and reconfigured to any size or shape space. And by

By lifting the plane of the farm, the designers created intimate, shaded areas below. Termed the Funderneath, the area held a wide range of practical and evocative programming.

———

The installation divided the courtyard into two large landscape rooms, with the porous boundary of the support columns creating smaller places beneath the farm.

236

EDIBLE LANDSCAPES

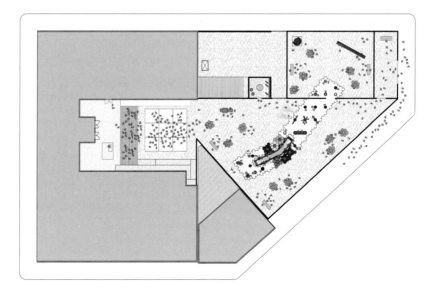

elevating the farm, the designers effectively doubled the size of the project, creating opportunities for urban activity below the farm surface. The farm's acreage provided shelter from sun and rain, while the columns provided nodes of activity, from seating to a cell phone charging station to a juice bar. The dynamic design not only demonstrated the potential of urban farming but also created a social space in which to learn about farming, play, and gather as a community.

The farm was made of forty-two "daisy" modules: six cut-off cardboard tubes of three different sizes (36 inches, 30 inches, and 28 inches—90, 76, and 71 centimeters—in diameter) clustered around a seventh tube. The outer ring of tubes—the petals—held soil cells planted with herbs, vegetables, and edible flowers, while the innermost tube either rested on a cardboard column or was left open for farm access from beneath. Each column, in addition to supporting the elevated farm, also organized the program beneath the farm. The twenty columns held seating; distribution points for produce, juice, and electricity; a periscope to view the farm above; sound and video recordings of farm animals; and fans.

Each daisy was planted in a single crop, selected to ensure color, fragrance, and produce throughout the summer. To harvest the produce, volunteers wore "picking skirts"—fabric that wrapped the volunteer's waist and connected to the daisy center, creating a receptacle for the produce. The skirts freed the volunteers' hands, allowing them to pop up through the central tube, place picked crops into the pouchlike skirt, and climb back down. The produce grown was used in the museum café, foraged by visitors, distributed to volunteers, and used at special events.

The urban farm was intended to be a closed-loop system. A rainwater collection system gathered and distributed more than 6,000 gallons into the drip irrigation system. All power needs—the irrigation system, pump and filtration for the pool, the juicers and cell phone charging station, and the lights and speakers—were served by solar panels; any excess power that was generated charged a battery array to provide reserve power for gray days. And because the installation was temporary, the designers ensured that all materials were biodegradable, recyclable, and easily demountable.

The elevated plane of the farm allowed a wide range of programming to occur in the shaded space beneath. This efficient use of space is a valuable model for urban sites.

Planter tubes playfully clustered around an open central tube from which volunteers could maintain the plants or harvest produce.

The farm grew a wide range of crops, herbs, and flowers to ensure production and vibrant color throughout the summer.

238

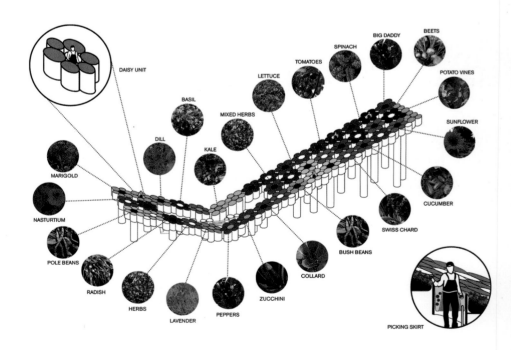

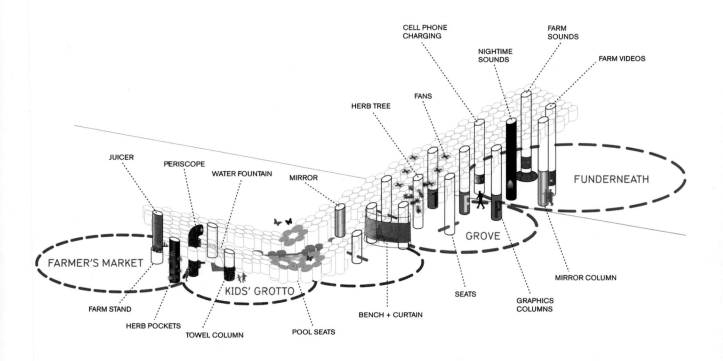

CELL PHONE CHARGING

FARM SOUNDS

NIGHTIME SOUNDS

FARM VIDEOS

FANS

HERB TREE

FUNDERNEATH

JUICER

PERISCOPE

WATER FOUNTAIN

MIRROR

FARMER'S MARKET

GROVE

KIDS' GROTTO

FARM STAND

MIRROR COLUMN

HERB POCKETS

SEATS

GRAPHICS COLUMNS

TOWEL COLUMN

POOL SEATS

BENCH + CURTAIN

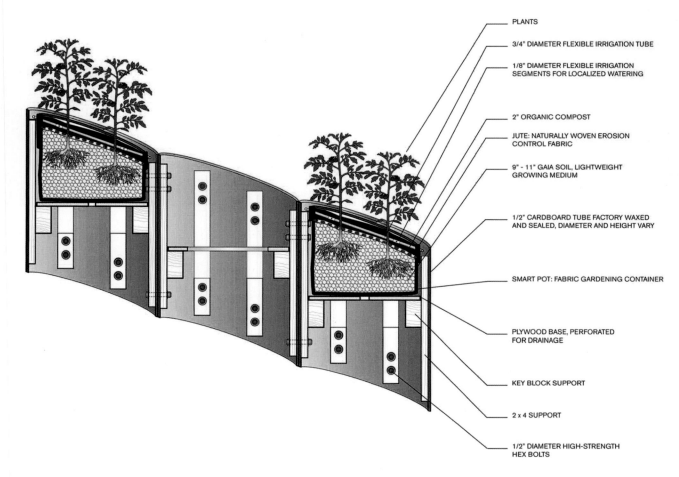

PLANTS

3/4" DIAMETER FLEXIBLE IRRIGATION TUBE

1/8" DIAMETER FLEXIBLE IRRIGATION SEGMENTS FOR LOCALIZED WATERING

2" ORGANIC COMPOST

JUTE: NATURALLY WOVEN EROSION CONTROL FABRIC

9" - 11" GAIA SOIL, LIGHTWEIGHT GROWING MEDIUM

1/2" CARDBOARD TUBE FACTORY WAXED AND SEALED, DIAMETER AND HEIGHT VARY

SMART POT: FABRIC GARDENING CONTAINER

PLYWOOD BASE, PERFORATED FOR DRAINAGE

KEY BLOCK SUPPORT

2 x 4 SUPPORT

1/2" DIAMETER HIGH-STRENGTH HEX BOLTS

The highly adaptable, modular system allows, in theory at least, an urban farm to be constructed rapidly, adapted to any site as it becomes available, and removed and reconfigured at another site. This idea of pop-up farming could allow urban farmers to take advantage of temporary site vacancies, short-term land leases, and existing rooftops.

The modular system also allows a second major innovation in urban agriculture, in its use of the section. By raising the urban farm on columns, P.F.1 created an urban environment beneath the farm. At P.F.1, programming beneath the structure included a farmers market, a kids' grotto, a pool, the Grove (a seating and socializing area), and the Funderneath (an area meant to bring the sound and images of a rural farm into the city). These various zones contained a juicer, a water fountain, pool seating, a periscope, mirror columns, swings, curtains, an herb tree, fans, a cell phone charging station, and nighttime sounds and farm sounds tubes. The wide range of activities for individuals and groups made P.F.1 a vibrant, playful community destination.

Public Farm 1 addressed serious concerns through playful design. Whimsical activities, carnival colors, and an air of performance art made the project an extremely successful summer festival site. Accessible materials, modular design, and low-tech construction made the project a viable model for urban farmers in nearly any city. Most striking, however, is the radical notion posited by P.F.1 that food production can be urbane, while urban centers can produce food.

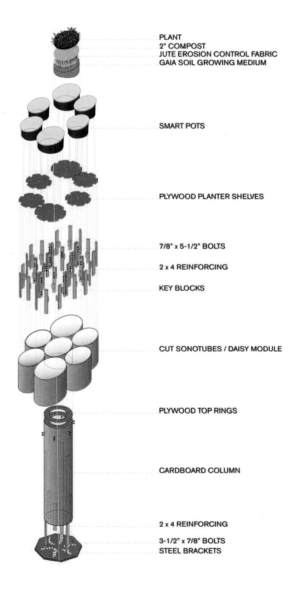

PLANT
2" COMPOST
JUTE EROSION CONTROL FABRIC
GAIA SOIL GROWING MEDIUM

SMART POTS

PLYWOOD PLANTER SHELVES

7/8" x 5-1/2" BOLTS

2 x 4 REINFORCING

KEY BLOCKS

CUT SONOTUBES / DAISY MODULE

PLYWOOD TOP RINGS

CARDBOARD COLUMN

2 x 4 REINFORCING

3-1/2" x 7/8" BOLTS
STEEL BRACKETS

Public Farm 1 explores modular construction in urban agriculture and, like the Hypar Pavilion, the possibilities of peeling urban landscape architecture off the ground to create inhabitable space beneath.

The modular daisy system was built from cardboard tubes; six smaller sections were bolted to a central column. The daisies combined to form a floating carpet of produce.

**241**

**Public open space in a business/residential district, comprising thirteen food-producing plazas connected by bike and pedestrian routes**

———

**LUXEMBOURG CITY, LUXEMBOURG**

**DESIGNED BY**
OKRA landscape architects
(Utrecht, the Netherlands)

**COMPLETED IN 2010**

**7 ACRES / 2.8 HECTARES**

# GRÜNEWALD PUBLIC ORCHARD

In the rapidly developing Kirchberg district of Luxembourg City, OKRA landscape architects designed an urban orchard to create continuity in the district amidst a variety of architectural styles and to foster neighborhood identity in a new development. The orchard creates a continuous landscape vocabulary to connect an office zone through a residential area to a large park to the south. A gradient of trees and ground covers provides wayfinding and placemaking block by block through the three zones. More than

Ripe pears draw attention to the unusual plant palette in the fragmented orchard. Fruits, nuts, and berries provide wayfinding in a residential district.

———

simple orientation through planting, this project asserts the radical notion that walking through an orchard, picking an apple, is a normal urban experience.

The Kirchberg Plateau, in northeast Luxembourg City, is the site of several European Union institutions—buildings housing multinational organizations such as the Secretariat of the European Parliament, built in 1966. Since the 1960s, the 900-acre (365-hectare) district has expanded rapidly, largely around these institutions. The plateau is divided into five quarters; the Grünewald quarter, named after the nearby Grünewald Forest, lies in the southeast of the plateau. In 2007, a competition called for a landscape plan for the district to unify the new development of five commercial and twenty-one residential buildings. The district plan designated a line of commercial blocks to the north, a checkerboard of medium-density residential blocks in the middle of the district, and a park to the south. Using food production to unify the neighborhood, OKRA landscape architects designed a network of thirteen plazas connected by north-south pedestrian and bike routes.

The designers call the project a fragmented orchard: pockets of production linked by a neutral gridded ground. The orchard provides a single unifying aesthetic and idea while also operating as an orienting device; its character varies depending on the context, providing residents with multisensory cues to their location. The neighborhood contains three orchard zones: in the northern office space, the reinterpreted orchard has flowering trees; in the central residential blocks, the productive orchard is planted with fruit trees; and in the south, adjacent to Klosegroendchen Park, the wild orchard has a natural aesthetic. Food production is focused in the tree canopy; the ground plane focuses on orientation through color and

The Grünewald Public Orchard unifies a neighborhood through a continuous productive landscape. Trees and shrubs produce a variety of fruits, nuts, and berries, as colors range from purples to oranges.

EDIBLE LANDSCAPES

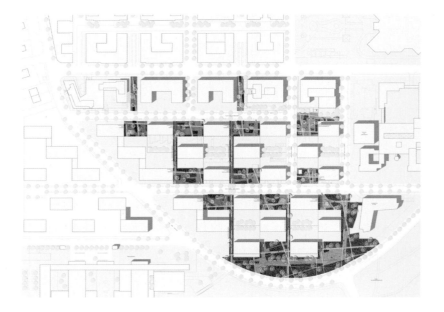

| LE VERGER REINTERPRETE | | LE VERGER DE PRODUCTION | | LE VERGER RUSTIQUE | | | |
|---|---|---|---|---|---|---|---|
| **1** | **2** | **3** | **4** | **5** | **6** | **7** | **8** |
| Prunus serrulata | Prunus serrulata | Prunus perzika | Sorbus aucuparia | Sorbus aucuparia | Sorbus aucuparia | Sorbus aucuparia | Sorbus aucuparia |
| Cercis siliquastrum | Cercis siliquastrum | Punus domestica | Sorbus torminalis | Sorbus torminalis | Juglans | Acer campestre | Prunus avium |
| Cercis canadensis | Cercis canadensis | Cydonia oblonga | Juglans regia | Juglans regia | Acer campestre | Juglans regia | Corylus avellana |
| Robinia | Liquidambar styraciflua | Malus domestica | Mespilus germanica | Corylus avellana | Amelanch | Cornus sang. | Cornus sang. |
| Magnolias | | Pyrus calleryana | | | | | Euonymus Europaeus |
| | | Prunus dulcis | | | | | |

texture, with a mixture of grassed and flowering areas. The plant palette shifts from purples in the north through reds and pinks in the center to oranges and yellows in the south. Each of the thirteen public courtyards, while being a recognizable member of a cohesive system, also offers an individual experience.

Tree varieties include apple, pear, hazelnut, walnut, and cherry, providing fruits and nuts through the seasons. These productive trees are mixed with more decorative trees, including locust and sweetgum, providing color and fragrance that enrich the visitor's sensory experience of the edible city. In the courtyards, trees are pruned in the round, while along the connecting paths, trees are espaliered; their distinct structure provides another form of wayfinding. The espaliered trees point the way through the narrow circulation zones, directing bicycle and pedestrian traffic along the primary north-south routes.

In the Grünewald Public Orchard, food production is used as a fully integrated urban strategy. Unlike in many urban agriculture projects, the productive landscape is not relegated to a discrete zone but is instead a continuous fabric, horizontally integrated with the decorative and recreational landscape fabric. As at P.F.1, food production is conceived as potentially urbane; crushed basalt paving, concrete paving strips, and concrete curbs and benches give the district a crisply elegant feel. The benches contain integrated lights under the lip of the seat that create a welcoming environment in the evening hours when most urban

Trees and shrubs are organized by productivity and color, creating an ever-shifting gradient of fruit and flowers.

The representational orchard is planted primarily in vibrant, colorful flowering trees and shrubs.

The productive orchard contains fruiting trees and shrubs.

The wild orchard takes cues from the adjacent Klosegroendchen Park and contains nut and fruit trees such as serviceberry with more habitat value than human value.

agriculture sites have closed their gates. Fruit and nut trees—the fragmented orchard—fit into this system, as do perennial planting beds and lawns. The designers have reinserted food production as part of the urban experience rather than isolating it as an anti-urban *hortus conclusus*.

The fragmented orchard negotiates the tension implicit in the term *urban agriculture*. It suggests that the urban can be agricultural, and vice versa. While food production is limited, it is also fully urban. There are some precedents for edible landscapes, such as the residential development of Village Homes in Davis, California (begun in 1975). There, the green infrastructure of paths, parks, and sidewalks is structured with quince hedges, fruit trees, and vineyards; the landscape is fully productive and edible. But Village Homes has a continuously productive landscape from ground cover to hedges to trees, while the Grünewald Public Orchard limits production to select plazas and paths. However, unlike many community gardens, the orchard is fully integrated into an urban context, as part of a plaza, not a set-aside district. And while Village Homes is a suburban community with an agricultural focus, Grünewald is a very urban setting that also provides food. The project falls strongly on the urban end of the spectrum, providing a precedent for cities that provide food for those who need or want it.

The orchard also raises questions. What is the quality of the produce; is it affected by the urban context? How are the trees maintained to ensure productivity? And without a dedicated group of farmers, will the produce be harvested, or will it be wasted as occurs in many cities with pears or plums as street trees? As further stages are built and the orchard matures, post-occupancy evaluations will answer those questions.

The trees, shrubs, and perennials provide vibrant color throughout the year, helping to orient residents in the new district.

Ground cover beds are a mix of flowering perennials, fruiting shrubs, and annual grains, here mixed with poppies and cornflowers.

Currants, peaches, and espaliered apples fill a continuously productive urban plaza.

———

Espaliered fruit trees along the main paths guide bicycle and pedestrian traffic.

# SOURCES AND REFERENCES

## INTRODUCTION: INDELIBLE SOCIAL MARKS

Freire, Paulo. 2000. *Pedagogy of the Oppressed*, 30th anniversary edition, trans. Myra Bergman Ramos. New York: Continuum.

Kwon, Miwon. 1997. One place after another: Notes on site specificity. *October* 80: 85–110.

Meyer, Elizabeth. 2006. From style to substance: Replacing the sight of architecture with the sites of architecture. UVa Architecture Forum, May 13.

## INFRASTRUCTURE: RETHINKING PUBLIC WORKS

Discussions of infrastructure design have included the 2008 University of Toronto symposium "Landscape infrastructures—Emerging practices, paradigms and technologies reshaping the contemporary urban landscape," the 2012 Harvard GSD symposium "Events: Landscape infrastructure," *Landscape Infrastructure: Case Studies by SWA* (2010), and the themed journals *Lotus 139: Landscape Infrastructures* (2009) and *Scenario 04: Rethinking Infrastructure* (2013).

Olmsted, Frederick Law. 1886. Paper on the Back Bay problem and its solution. In *The Papers of Frederick Law Olmsted: Supplementary Series Vol. 1, Writings on Public Parks, Parkways, and Park Systems*, ed. Charles E. Beveridge and Carolyn R. Hoffman, pp. 437–60. Baltimore: Johns Hopkins University Press, 1997.

Shannon, Kelly. 2010. *The Landscape of Contemporary Infrastructure*. Rotterdam: NAi Publishers.

Strang, Gary L. 1996. Infrastructure as landscape. *Places* 10 (3): 8–15.

### Moses Bridge at Fort de Roovere

Benezra, Neal, I. Michael Danoff, M. Jessica Rowe, et al. 1998. *An Uncommon Vision: The Des Moines Art Center*. New York: Hudson Hills Press.

Miss, Mary, Daniel M. Abramson, et al. 2004. *Mary Miss*. New York: Princeton Architectural Press.

West Brabantse Waterlinie. http://www.westbrabantsewaterlinie.nl/

### Queens Plaza

Gardner, Ralph, Jr. 2012. In Queens, an artistic alteration. Urban Gardener, *Wall Street Journal*, July 23.

New York City Department of Design and Construction and the Design Trust for Public Space. 2005. *High Performance Infrastructure Guidelines*. http://www.nyc.gov/html/ddc/downloads/pdf/hpig.pdf

Ruddick, Margie. 2013. Queens Plaza: A new core for Long Island City. *Scenario 03: Rethinking Infrastructure* (Spring).

Yoneda, Yuka. 2011. Queens Plaza to be transformed into a vibrant green oasis in Long Island City. Inhabitat, March 10. http://inhabitat.com/nyc/queens-plaza-to-be-transformed-into-a-vibrant-green-oasis-in-long-island-city/

### Solar Strand

Brake, Alan G. 2010. Electric landscape: Water Hood fuses solar array into new U. Buffalo open space. The Architect's Newspaper, April 22. http://archpaper.com/news/articles.asp?id=4449

Fischer, Anne. 2013. University's Solar Strand. Solar Novus Today, June 22. http://www.solarnovus.com/universitys-solar-strand_N6680.html

Scognamiglio, Alessandra. 2012. Solar Strand. *Domus*: 75–78.

———. 2013. The Solar Strand: Interview with Robert G. Shibley. Domus online. http://www.domusweb.it/en/interviews/2013/09/02/forms_of_energy_.html

Shibley, Robert, Dennis Black, Ryan McPherson, and James R Simon. 2012. Culture clash: Art, electrons, teaching, research, and engagement meet at the Solar Strand. AASHE Case Study, June 29. http://www.aashe.org/resources/case-studies/culture-clash-art-electrons-teaching-researchand-engagement-meet-solar-strand

Slessor, Catherine. 2010. Energy in the landscape: Turning a solar array on a US college campus into land art. *Architectural Review* 228: 38.

UB Now. 2010. International Competition for Solar Project. http://www.youtube.com/watch?v=9sCJ9RNvtBg

### Coastal Levees and Lone Star Coastal National Recreation Area

Archie, Michelle L., and Howard D. Terry. 2011. *Opportunity Knocks: How the Proposed Lone Star Coastal National Recreation Area Could Attract Visitors, Boost Business, and Create Jobs*. Washington, DC: National Parks Conservation Association.

Bedient, Dr. Philip B., Jim Blackburn, and Antonia Sebastian. 2011. *SSPEED Center Phase 1 Report: Learning the Lessons of Hurricane Ike: Preparing for the Next Big One*. Houston, TX: SSPEED Center.

Errick, Jennifer. 2012. A new model for parks could help revitalize Texas' Gulf Coast. *NPCA's Park Advocate*, May 11. http://www.parkadvocate.org/?p=130

National Parks Conservation Association. 2012. Lone Star Coastal National Recreation Area. http://www.npca.org/exploring-our-parks/slideshows/lone-star-coastal.html/ http://www.npca.org/about-us/regional-offices/texas/lone-star/

Sass, Ron. 2012. An ecological perspective on the proposed Lone Star Coastal National Recreation Area. SSPEED Conference, Gulf Coast Hurricanes: Mitigation and Response, April 10.

Yoskowitz, David W., James Gibeaut, and Ali McKenzie. 2009. *The Socio-Economic Impact of Sea Level Rise in the Galveston Bay Region*. A report for Environmental Defense Fund. Harte Research Institute for Gulf of Mexico Studies, Texas A&M University, June.

## POSTINDUSTRIAL LANDSCAPES: RECLAIMING SITES OF INDUSTRY

Eisenman, Peter. 1987. Architecture and the problem of the rhetorical figure. *Architecture and Urbanism* 7 (202): 15–80.

Latz, Peter. 1993. "Design" by handling the existing. In *Modern Park Design: Recent Trends*. Amsterdam: Thoth.

Meyer, Elizabeth K. 1997. The expanded field of landscape architecture. In *Ecological Design and Planning*, ed. George F. Thompson and Frederick R. Steiner, p. 52. New York: Wiley, 1997.

Smithson, Robert. 1971. The Earth, subject to cataclysms, is a cruel master. Interview with Gregoire Müller, in *Robert Smithson, The Collected Writings*, ed. Jack Flam, p. 256. Berkeley: University of California Press, 1996.

### Paddington Reservoir Gardens

Hawken, Scott. 2011. Paddington Reservoir—a new public space for Sydney: A focus on design and reuse turned the former Paddington Reservoir into an outstanding park—an urban counterpoint to the city's range of harbourside landscapes. *Topos: The International Review of Landscape Architecture and Urban Design* 77: 78–83.

Leigh, Gweneth Newman. 2010. Chamber music: In Sydney, a 19th-century reservoir qualifies as an antiquity—Now it's a fascinating city park. *Landscape Architecture* 100(12): 78–89.

### Jaffa Landfill Park

Braudo, Alisa. 2010. Reconnecting the Tel-Aviv Jaffa shoreline between Reading Park and Jaffa Landfill Park, Israel. *Topos: The International Review of Landscape Architecture and Urban Design* 72: 74–79.

Goldhaber, Ravit. 2010. The Jaffa Slope project: An analysis of "Jaffaesque" narratives in the new millennium. *Makan: Adalah's Journal for Land, Planning and Justice* 2: 47–69.

### Haute Deûle River Banks

Dickinson, Robert Eric. 1951. *The West European City: A Geographical Interpretation*, Lille, pp. 132–36. London: Routledge & Paul.

Ministère de l'Écologie, du Développement Durable, des Transports et du Logement. January 2011. Palmarès EcoQuartier 2009: Eau—EcoQuartier les rives de la Haute-Deûle, villes de Lille et Lomme.

### Northala Fields

Coulthard, Tim. 2009. Northala Fields forever: Northala Fields, the largest park to be built in London for a century, is an exemplar of sustainable construction and design. *Landscape Architecture* 99 (5): 94–101.

Fink, Peter. 2007. Politics and the park. *Green Places* 32: 20–23.

## VEGETATED ARCHITECTURE: LIVING ROOFS AND WALLS

### European Environment Agency

Edwards, Brian. 2010. A blossoming installation contributes to a city's wider ecological diversity. A10.eu: New European Architecture, 4 August. http://www.a10.eu/news/meanwhile/living_facade_copenhagen.html

European Environment Agency. 2010. Europe in bloom: A living facade at the European Environment Agency. http://www.eea.europa.eu/events/

Lushe. 2010. Living map on Copenhagen wall. Lushe website, 25 May. http://www.lushe.com.au/living-map-on-copenhagen-wall/

### Hypar Pavilion

Hypar Pavilion in New York. 2011. *Detail* 51(10): 1182–85.

### Park TMB

Gali-Izard, Teresa. 2004. Park over the TMB bus depot in Horta. *Quaderns d-arquitectura I urbanisme* (October): 63.

Garden over the Horta Bus Depot, Barcelona. 2007. *Patent Constructions: New Architecture Made in Catalonia*, ed. Albert Ferre, pp. 224–27. Barcelona: Actar.

Hypostyle garden. 2007. *Patent Constructions: New Architecture Made in Catalonia*, ed. Albert Ferre, pp. 228–37. Barcelona: Actar.

Krauel, Jacobo. 2008. Park over the Horta Bus Depot. *Urban Spaces: New City Parks*, pp. 18–31. Barcelona: Carles Broto.

Parc TMB: Barcelona (Spain), 2006. 2012. Public Space. http://www.publicspace.org/en/print-works/e009-parc-tmb

Park on the roof of Horta Bus Depot. 2008. *El Croquis*: 178–87.

Parque TMB, Barcelona. 2006. *A + T*: 64–77.

## Seymour-Capilano Filtration Plant

Takaoka, S., and F. J. Swanson. 2008. Change in extent of meadows and shrub fields in the central western Cascade Range, Oregon. *The Professional Geographer* 60(4): 1–14.

Teensma, P.D.A., J. T. Rienstra, and M. A. Yelter. 1991. Preliminary reconstruction and analysis of change in forest stand age classes of the Oregon Coast Range from 1850 to 1940. USDI Bureau of Land Management Technical Note T/N OR-9.

## ECOLOGICAL URBANISM: DESIGN INFORMED BY NATURAL SYSTEMS

Amidon, Jane. 2010. Big Nature. In *Design Ecologies: Essays on the Nature of Design*, ed. Lisa Tilder and Beth Blostein, p. 180. New York: Princeton Architectural Press.

Chris Maser. 2009. Nature's inviolate principles. *Social-Environmental Planning: The Design Interface Between Everyforest and Everycity*. Boca Raton, FL: CRC Press.

Mohsen Mostafavi. 2011. Why ecological urbanism? Why now? In *Ecological Urbanism*, ed. Mohsen Mostafavi and Gareth Doherty. Baden: Lars Müller Publishers.

Olmsted, Frederick Law. 1886. Paper on the Back Bay problem and its solution. In *The Papers of Frederick Law Olmsted: Supplementary Series Vol. 1, Writings on Public Parks, Parkways, and Park Systems*, ed. Charles E. Beveridge and Carolyn R. Hoffman, pp. 437–60. Baltimore: Johns Hopkins University Press, 1997.

Terry Tempest Williams. 2001. *Red: Passion and Patience in the Desert*, p. 75. New York: Pantheon.

## Teardrop Park

Beardsley, John, Janice Ross, and Randy Gragg. 2009. *Where the Revolution Began: Lawrence and Anna Halprin and the Reinvention of Public Space*, p. 16. Washington, DC: Spacemaker Press.

de Jong, Erik. 2009. Teardrop Park: Elective affinities. In *Michael Van Valkenburgh Associates: Reconstructing Urban Landscapes*, ed. Anita Berrizbeitia. New Haven: Yale University Press.

Gould, Stephen Jay. 1991. Unenchanted evening. *Natural History* 100(9): 6–7.

Heerwagen, Judith. 2009. Biophilia, health, and well-being. In *Restorative Commons: Creating Health and Well-being through Urban Landscapes*, ed. Lindsay Campbell and Anne Wiesen, pp. 39–57. US Forest Service, Northern Research Station, General Technical Report NRS-P-39.

Hines, Susan. 2007. Abstract realism. *Landscape Architecture Magazine* (February): 94–103.

Moore, Robin. 2007. Reasons to smile at Teardrop. *Landscape Architecture* 97(12): 134–36.

Stegner, Peter. 2009. Teardrop Park [Battery Park City, New York]. *Topos: The International Review of Landscape Architecture & Urban Design*, 67: 29–34.

Teardrop Park. 2010. Landscape Architecture Foundation Case Study Brief. http://www.lafoundation.org/research/landscape-performance-series/case-studies/case-study/391/

## Péage Sauvage

Clément, Gilles. 2003. The Third Landscape. http://www.gillesclement.com/cat-tierspaysage-tit-le-Tiers-Paysage

## Buffalo Bayou

American Planning Association. 2012. Great Places in American: Public Spaces. http://www.planning.org/greatplaces/spaces/characteristics.htm

Broto, Carles. 2013. *Urban Spaces: Design and Innovation*. Barcelona: Links Books.

Hung, Ying-Yu, Gerdo Aquino, Charles Waldheim, and Pierre Bélanger. 2013. *Landscape Infrastructure: Case Studies by SWA*, second and revised edition. Basel: Birkhäuser.

Jost, Daniel. 2009. Under the interstate. *Landscape Architecture* 99(10): 78–86.

Lockwood, Charles. 2006. Bagby-to-Sabine: A new beginning. UrbanLand (October): 110–13.

Ozil, Taner R., Sameepa Modi, and Dylan Stewart. 2013. Buffalo Bayou Promenade. Landscape Architecture Foundation Landscape Performance Series case study.

Shanley, Kevin. 2009. Houston's Buffalo Bayou Promenade. *Parks and Recreation* 44(5): 18–23.

———. 2009. Infrastructure as amenity: Houston's bayou becomes a floodway-turned-park. *Topos* 69: 32–37.

Shanley, Kevin, and James Vick. 2010. Spreading risk and reward. UrbanLand, September 28. http://urbanland.uli.org/economy-markets-trends/spreading-risk-and-reward/

Sieber, Ann Walton. 2006. A pleasant promenade: A new pathway along the banks of Buffalo Bayou hopes to remind the city of its liquid assets. *Cite* 66 (Spring): 9–10.

Sokol, David. 2007. Buffalo Bayou, Houston. *Architectural Record* 195(5): 285–86.

Urban Land Institute. 2008. Sabine-to-Bagby Promenade. ULI Development Case Studies.

## EDIBLE LANDSCAPES: AGRICULTURE IN THE CITY

American Society for Horticultural Science. 2009. Conserving historic apple trees. ScienceDaily, November 10.

Campbell, Lindsay, and Anne Wiesen, eds. 2009. *Restorative Commons: Creating Health and Well-being through Urban Landscapes*. US Forest Service, Northern Research Station, General Technical Report NRS-P-39.

Canning, Patrick, Ainsley Charles, Sonya Huang, Karen R. Polenske, and Arnold Waters. 2010. *Energy Use in the U.S. Food System*. USDA Economic Research Report Number 94.

Cockrall-King, Jennifer. 2012. *Food and the City: Urban Agriculture and the New Food Revolution*. Amherst, NY: Prometheus Books.

de la Salle, Janine, Mark Holland, eds. 2010. Agricultural Urbanism: Handbook for Building Sustainable Food Systems in 21st Century Cities. Winnepeg, Manitoba: Green Frigate Books.

Gorgolewski, Mark, June Komisar, and Joe Nasr. 2011. *Carrot City: Creating Places for Urban Agriculture*. New York: Monacelli Press.

Hodgson, Kimberley, Marcia Caton Campbell, and Martin Bailkey. 2011. *Urban Agriculture: Growing Healthy, Sustainable Places*. American Planning Association, Planning Advisory Service, Report Number 563.

Hou, Jeffrey, Julie M. Johnson, and Laura J. Lawson. 2009. *Greening Cities, Growing Communities: Learning from Seattle's Urban Community Gardens*. Seattle: University of Washington Press.

Lawson, Laura J. 2005. *City Bountiful: A Century of Community Gardening in America*. Berkeley: University of California Press.

Lawson, Laura, and Luke Drake. 2012. *Community Gardening Organization Survey 2011–2012*. American Community Gardening Association, Rutgers School of Environmental and Biological Sciences.

Martinez, Steve, et al. 2010. *Local Food Systems: Concepts, Impacts, and Issues*. USDA Economic Research Report Number 97.

Monroe-Santos, Suzanne, et al. 2008. National Community Gardening Survey: 1996. American Community Gardening Association. http://communitygarden.org/learn/resources/publications.php

Nordahl, Darrin. 2009. *Public Produce: The New Urban Agriculture*. Washington, DC: Island Press.

Pirog, Rich, and Andrew Benjamin. 2003. Checking the food odometer: Comparing food miles for local versus conventional produce sales to Iowa institutions. Leopold Center for Sustainable Agriculture, Ames, IA.

Steel, Carolyn. 2009. *Hungry City: How Food Shapes Our Lives*. London: Vintage Books.

## Gary Comer Youth Center Roof Garden

Flood, Ann. 2009. Visiting the Gary Comer Youth Center's rooftop garden. The Local Beet, Chicago edition, July 22. http://www.thelocalbeet.com/2009/07/22/visiting-the-gary-comer-youth-center's-rooftop-garden/

Gorgolewski, Mark, June Komisar, and Joe Nasr. 2011. *Carrot City: Creating Places for Urban Agriculture*. New York: Monacelli Press.

Hockenberry, John. 2006. Miracle on 72nd Street. *Metropolis* magazine, December. http://www.metropolismag.com/December-2006/Miracle-on-72nd-Street/

Killory, Christine. 2008. *Detail in Process*. New York: Princeton Architectural Press.

Reinwald, Pete. 2010. Comer Youth Center project is a garden in the desert. *Chicago Tribune*, August 11.

Ronan, John. 2010. *Explorations: The Architecture of John Ronan*. New York: Princeton Architectural Press.

## Beacon Food Forest

Beacon Food Forest Permaculture Project. http://beaconfoodforest.org

Mellinger, Robert. 2012. Nation's largest public food forest takes root on Beacon Hill. Crosscut, February 16. http://crosscut.com/2012/02/16/agriculture/21892/Nations-largest-public-Food-Forest-takes-root-on-B/

Thompson, Claire. 2012. Into the woods: Seattle plants a public food forest. Grist, February 28. http://grist.org/urban-agriculture/into-the-woods-seattle-plants-a-public-food-forest/

Valdes, Manuel. 2012. Construction will start in June on Jefferson Park "food forest." Seattle Daily Journal of Commerce, March 8. https://www.djc.com/news/en/12038680.html

## Public Farm 1

Andraos, Amale, and Dan Wood, eds. 2010. *Above the Pavement—the Farm! Architecture and Agriculture at PF1*. New York: Princeton Architectural Press.

Gorgolewski, Mark, June Komisar, and Joe Nasr. 2011. *Carrot City: Creating Places for Urban Agriculture*, pp. 104–09. New York: Monacelli Press.

Tilder, Lisa. 2010. *Design Ecologies: Essays on the Nature of Design*. New York: Princeton Architectural Press.

# ACKNOWLEDGMENTS

I am truly thankful for the many forms of assistance I have received from so many people as I have written this book. Without them, I would have had no projects to write about, fewer images to show, less elegant text, and a nearly impossible task of bringing the book to completion.

The twenty-five projects showcased here are the result of tremendous creativity, expertise, and dedication from a very large number of designers, artists, engineers, clients, and others. They are too many to name, but I am grateful for their vision, and I am indebted to the firms and photographers who shared project images and discussed the work with me. You are changing the profession. Thank you.

My colleagues have assisted me throughout this project, from reading project proposals and critiquing case studies to reviewing text. I am particularly grateful to James Harper for frequent review of the work; Matt Potteiger for insights on urban agriculture; Kenny Helphand and Liska Chan for case study suggestions; and Beth Meyer for connecting me with Juree Sondker. Amanda Ingmire and Sophia Duluk were research assistants on the urban agriculture and vegetated architecture chapters; those chapters are stronger and more diverse for their work. Andrew Louw was research assistant on a Landscape Architecture Foundation case study of Queens Plaza; much of the excellent detail on that project comes from his fieldwork. And Leah Erickson managed the Herculean task of collecting images and image permissions for most of the projects; the book is more informative and engaging because of her work.

Timber Press has been a pleasure to work with on this project. Andrew Beckman reviewed the text, and his feedback helped shape the book. Lorraine Anderson clarified my thoughts and strengthened the threads weaving the text together. Juree Sondker clarified the scope and vision of the book, sent words of encouragement, and wrested text from me when necessary. Thank you.

# IMAGE CREDITS

# INDEX

Illustrations are indexed according to the page number of the caption.